Teaching Psychology in Secondary Schools

by

RICHARD A. KASSCHAU

and

MICHAEL WERTHEIMER

Andrew S. Thomas Memorial Library
MORRIS HARVEY COLLEGE, CHARLESTON, W. VA

Published jointly by

American Psychological Association
1200 Seventeenth Street, N.W.
Washington, D.C. 20036

ERIC Clearinghouse for Social Studies/
Social Science Education
855 Broadway
Boulder, Colorado 80302

Published in 1974 by

American Psychological Association
1200 Seventeenth Street, N.W., Washington, D.C. 20036

and

ERIC Clearinghouse for Social Studies/
Social Science Education
855 Broadway, Boulder, Colorado 80302

The material in this publication was prepared pursuant to a contract with the National Institute of Education, U.S. Department of Health, Education, and Welfare. Contractors undertaking such projects under government sponsorship are encouraged to express freely their judgment in professional and technical matters. Prior to publication, the manuscript was submitted to the American Psychological Association for critical review and determination of professional competence. Points of view or opinions, however, do not necessarily represent the official view or opinions of either the American Psychological Association or the National Institute of Education.

This publication is one in a series on trends in social science education being developed by ERIC/ChESS. Others in the series are:

Pulliam, W. *The status of world history instruction in American secondary schools.* (1972, ERIC/ChESS)
Turner, M. J. *The status of political science instruction in American secondary schools.* (1974, ERIC/ChESS-SSEC)
Vuicich, G., & Stoltman, J. *Geography in elementary and secondary education: Tradition to opportunity.* (1974, ERIC/ChESS-SSEC)

A parallel series is designed to give teachers practical suggestions on innovative teaching strategies and materials in the social sciences. Publications in this series are:

Bare, J. K. *Psychology: Where to begin.* (1971, ERIC/ChESS-APA)
Helburn, S. W. *Preparing to teach economics: Sources and approaches.* (1971, ERIC/ChESS)
Turner, M. J. *Preparing to teach political science: Sources and approaches.* (1974, ERIC/ChESS-SSEC)

APA Production

　　OFFICE OF EDUCATIONAL AFFAIRS: Margo Johnson.
　　OFFICE OF COMMUNICATIONS: Harold P. Van Cott, Director; Elliot R. Siegel, Executive Editor for Separate Publications; Elizabeth Forrester, Editor; Patricia Walsh, Editor.

Printed in the United States of America

Table of Contents

PREFACE	v
ACKNOWLEDGMENT	viii
ABOUT THE AUTHORS	viii
INTRODUCTION	1
HISTORY OF THE ENDEAVOR	3
The Nineteenth Century	3
From 1900 to 1940	3
From 1940 to 1960	4
The 1960s	5
Recent Trends	7
Recent Survey Results	10
PHILOSOPHY	13
The Context	13
Goals	15
Issues	16
Personal Development	18
Psychology as a Discipline	25
A Synthesis	31
PSYCHOLOGY CURRICULUM MATERIALS	37
Personal Development	37
Psychology as a Discipline	39
The Synthesis	41
Comment	43
Sources of Information	44
TEACHER TRAINING AND CERTIFICATION	45
Survey Results	45
Implications of the Three Philosophies for Teacher Preparation	47
Teacher Preparation	49
Some Model Training Curricula	50
Certification of Psychology Teachers	52
Summary	54
APPENDIX A	55
APPENDIX B	58
REFERENCES	59

DEDICATION

We dedicate *Teaching Psychology in Secondary Schools* to the late **Robert S. Fox**. This document was his doing—his ideals created it, his patience facilitated it, his perseverance brought it to fruition.
R.A.K. and M.W.

Preface

In the three decades since World War II, the field of psychology has grown to its present state of maturity as a unique and complex blend of facts, perspectives, and practices. Most of these have met with sufficient public acceptance to make psychology currently the largest single disciplinary producer of bachelor's degrees. Not surprisingly, there has been a parallel growth in psychology at precollege levels, predominantly in the high schools. The rapid growth of psychology at all educational levels is associated with the relatively recent mass popularization of psychology and some notable practical achievements that have arisen from that subject matter. The plethora of TV "experts," Sunday-supplement expositions on various psychological phenomena, self-help approaches to personal adjustment, bombardment by the visual media in both dramatic and documentary form with virtually every kind of psychological activity—all of these have fueled both a mass awareness and mass demand for more formal education in psychology, especially at the precollege level. The success of the magazine *Psychology Today* serves as an excellent illustration of this unassailable fact.

Educators at both the elementary and secondary levels have sensed the growth of this demand and are trying to meet it with the resources at their disposal. Virtually all teachers, whatever their ultimate specialty, have had a course or two in psychology. With the growth of more open and direct methods of instruction, particularly at the secondary level, and with the growing demand for psychological content, it is only natural that many secondary teachers have begun explicitly to teach psychology while continuing implicitly to "use" it in their teaching.

It is not surprising to find that efforts to teach psychology, particularly at the secondary level, mirror the broad range of preconceptions and approaches to the discipline that have for years characterized both teaching and practice at higher educational levels. Obviously, a college-level psychologist who attends a meeting of high school psychology teachers will be very much at home with the debates that rage: humanism versus behaviorism, science versus art, discipline orientation versus personal adjustment, and so on. These debates, after all, have occupied psychologists for nearly 30 years. They reflect the situation that has always prevailed when a science spawns a technology that must, for awhile, share bed and board with the parent.

There are, however, some significant differences between a gathering of college psychology professors and a gathering of high school teachers of psychology—an observation that brings us to the purpose of the present book. Whereas the college professor is a member of several discipline-oriented professional societies, the secondary school teacher has no such sources of professional identity. By tracing the growth and documenting the breadth of present-day psychology at the secondary school level, Kasschau and Wertheimer have taken an important step toward establishing a separate identity for high school psychology teachers. Because these authors are both distinguished psychologists in their own right, their work will be doubly effective in this regard. It will command the attention not only of those whose activities and aspirations it so eloquently describes, but also of others who must recognize and act upon the fact that psychology is taught in the high school and increasingly so.

A second distinction between college professors and high school teachers emerges from the practical, action-oriented approach of high school psychology teachers. They are doers, not talkers. They are willing to discuss the academic merits of the humanistic or behavioristic approach and participate in workshops that contrast discipline-oriented psychology with the personal-adjustment model. But when it comes to their own teaching, they are faced with having to find a working compromise between any such pair of polar opposites. Such a compromise, or synthesis, together with the thesis and antithesis from which it emerges, has been suggested by Kasschau and Wertheimer. Their synthesis, however, may also be taken as a testimonial to the new profession having fully arrived since, in suggesting it, these spokesmen for precollege psychology have made an invaluable contribution to the discipline as a whole.

For nearly two decades, the American Psychological Association has manifested awareness of and interest in the growth of psychology at the precollege level. Its Committee on Precollege Psychology, a subsidiary of the Education and Training Board, has actively attempted to define and keep pace with the growth without putting the Association on one or another side of the various issues (e.g., the place of psychology in the high school curriculum, certification of teachers, reforms in preservice training, and the like). In a real sense, the present book is a compendium of the knowledge gained by the Committee on Precollege Psychology over many years. In the context of the Association's commitment to place psychology squarely in the mainstream of the educational venture, this book is a tribute to the fact that the Association has recognized and is beginning to meet its responsibility.

We must hasten to point out, however, that this work is also representative of the ERIC Clearinghouse for Social Studies/Social Science Education (ERIC/ChESS), which seeks most effectively to collect and disseminate information about research and practice in the social sciences and social studies. In this, its second collaborative publication with the American Psychological Association, ERIC/ChESS is again demonstrating its sensitivity to the need for a periodic summary and dissemination of activities that would otherwise remain unpublicized. Through the efforts of ERIC/ChESS, the likelihood of periodic reinvention of the wheel is substantially reduced; the benefits of this service during a time of exploding knowledge can hardly be overestimated.

There are a number of people whose commitment and dedication on behalf of this project merit special recognition. The manuscript was thoroughly reviewed on two occasions by Ambrose Clegg of Kent State University, Raymond G. Hunt of Cornell University, and Richard Pitner, Teacher Associate at the Social Science Education Consortium in 1973-74, now at Kennedy High School, Cedar Rapids, Iowa. The late Robert S. Fox, director of ERIC/ChESS, initiated the project and supervised it along the way, ably assisted by ERIC/ChESS editors Karen Wiley and Chris Ahrens. Finally, the authors join me in acknowledging both the public and personal indebtedness of all those involved, not only with this volume, but with the entire precollege psychology enterprise, to James Russell Nazzaro and Margo Johnson of the Educational Affairs Office of the APA.

> H. S. Pennypacker, Chairman
> Committee on Precollege Psychology (1972 and 1973)
> American Psychological Association

ACKNOWLEDGMENT

The authors wish to express their sincere appreciation for the useful, astutely critical commentary on this document offered by Margo Johnson of the Educational Affairs Office, American Psychological Association. Her support was ever positive, her advice frequently sought and seldom ignored. As with so many things in precollege psychology, her contribution is present in this document. For the content we assume full responsibility; to the extent the discussion is reasonably coherent, we recognize with thanks the contribution of Ms. Johnson.

R.A.K and M.W.

ABOUT THE AUTHORS

Richard A. Kasschau received his PhD in experimental psychology from the University of Tennessee in 1967. He was a participant in the Oberlin Project (Program on the Teaching of Psychology in Secondary Schools) in 1970, and later directed a follow-up project at the University of South Carolina, where he has been an associate professor since 1971. On leave from U.S.C., he spent 1973-74 at the APA as a Washington Intern in Education. He is now serving as the Director of Undergraduate Studies in the Department of Psychology, University of Houston.

Michael Wertheimer received his PhD in experimental psychology from Harvard University in 1952. He served as President of APA Division Two in 1965, and is a former member, and past chairman, of the Committee on Precollege Psychology of the APA. In addition, he served as the acting administrative officer for Educational Affairs in 1970-71. Presently, he is a member of the Education and Training Board (APA), President-Elect of APA Division One, and Associate Director of the Center for Education in Social Sciences at the University of Colorado where he has been a professor since 1961.

Introduction

Psychology has been taught in United States schools, especially at the secondary level, since at least the 1830s. The growth in both numbers of students and courses was modest yet steady through the first half of the 20th century but has been particularly rapid during the last decade. It is now estimated that between one half and three quarters of a million students are enrolled in precollege psychology courses. Our attention in this document is limited primarily to high school psychology courses since this is where the increases in enrollment and the resultant increases in training and curriculum development activities are most dramatic.

The focal issue concerns not whether to teach psychology at precollege levels, but rather how best to do so. Who represents the primary audience for such courses — the collegebound student? The noncollegebound? What are the appropriate objectives for such a precollege course — personal adjustment of the students? Communication of the facts of psychology as a discipline? The issues are many; the answers are few, and frequently debated.

Precollege psychology is an area of rapid growth in student interest and enrollment, an area of substantial change and rich opportunity. The issues run deep, but interest is high, and the time has come for examining the philosophical assertions underlying teaching precollege psychology.

The teaching of psychology in United States schools is growing today at an accelerating pace, but it is by no means something entirely new. Psychology, in some form or another, has been taught in American schools for at least 140 years. A quarter of a century ago, perhaps one high school in 10 offered a course in psychology; in 1973 the figure was closer to one in every four or five; and the proportion continues to grow each year. There are now an estimated 10,000 people teaching psychology in high schools in the United States. Even a decade ago there were almost 150,000 high school students enrolled in psychology courses, at a time when there were only about 2,000 high school psychology teachers. This implies that there may well be over half a million or more high school students enrolled in psychology courses today.

At least four separate factors have influenced the growth of precollege psychology: educators, students, federal funding, and professional agencies. A major determinant, of course, is educators, particularly the social studies specialists who are constantly trying to make the school curriculum responsive both to the needs of the students and to the rapid changes in the knowledge base of the social sciences.

A second major force is the students themselves. The students' pleas for relevance in their school experiences have intensified at both the college and precollege levels, and they see psychology as potentially very useful for coping with the real world.

A third source of influence is the subtly changing deployment of national resources, such as government funding, via the National Science Foundation, the United States Office of Education, the National Institute of Education, and other agencies, to meet the shifting priorities of modern times. Massive infusions of federal funds have helped to change the direction of curriculum planning and implementation.

Finally, though perhaps with less impact, professional associations of various kinds have advanced the spirit of the times, getting educational practices to move in directions consistent with their ideals. Among these are societies of educators such as the National Council for the Social Studies and the National Education Association; discipline-centered societies such as the American Anthropological Association, the Association of American Geographers, the American Political Science Association, the American Psychological Association, and the American Sociological Association; and groups of educators and discipline-oriented people such as the Social Science Education Consortium, concerned with dissemination of curriculum information and implementation of new curriculum materials, or the now defunct Consortium of Professional Associations for Study of Special Teacher Improvement Programs.

These four determinants, and others that could be identified, operate within a complex social and historical matrix that forms the environment of the entire educational venture. In recent years this matrix has included such diverse features as accountability, cross-age and peer teaching, simulation/gaming, open schools, individualized instruction, vastly improved audiovisual support technology, behavioral objectives, the search for alternatives to the lecture method, micro-teaching, inquiry training, focus on the "whole child" with a commitment to affective as well as cognitive goals. Several of these tie in closely with the increase in psychological instruction at educational levels before college; others run counter to and tend to impede this growth.

The present document examines the teaching of psychology at levels below college. Many of the curriculum development efforts and most of the enrollment increases in precollege psychology courses have been focused at the secondary level. While our discussion includes efforts at elementary and junior high school levels, it is limited primarily to high school psychology courses. We begin with a brief history of the field and then document the rapid growth of the endeavor in recent years. Next, some of the philosophical issues behind the teaching of psychology at the elementary, junior high, and high school levels are considered. The last two sections are devoted to the primary areas in which these philosophical issues have an impact: instructional approaches and teacher training.

History of the Endeavor

The history of the teaching and growth of precollege psychology in the United States seems to fall into four eras. First, there was the 19th century, marked by little distinct growth or development but characterized by scattered activity. The early 20th century (1900-1940) saw the development of the discipline generally and its identification as a separate body of knowledge. Also, there were a number of attempts to gather data both on the nature of teaching efforts at precollege levels and the type of student enrolling in psychology courses. From 1940 to 1960 increased efforts were made at secondary school levels, including the publication of several textbooks especially for high school students. In addition, efforts were initiated during this period to introduce psychological content at the elementary and junior high levels. The period since 1960 has seen an accelerated growth of student interest and professional activities in the field.

THE NINETEENTH CENTURY

Unearthed in a collection of some 70 psychology-related textbooks, all published in the United States before 1890, were seven that were intended for use in secondary schools, though two of these were written for teachers rather than pupils (Louttit, 1956). Among the earliest was *Elements of Mental Philosophy*, a two-volume work by Thomas C. Upham originally published in 1831 and abridged to a single volume in 1840; the first edition was used in some secondary schools (Roback, 1952), and the second was expressly intended for academies and high schools. In 1840, Elizabeth Ricard's text based on lectures at the Geneva Female Seminary was published (Louttit, 1956), and there is evidence that a high school course in "mental philosophy" (which nowadays doubtlessly would have been called psychology) was officially on the books in St. Louis in 1857 (Coffield & Engle, 1960). In 1889 two texts clearly intended for secondary schools were published. They were *Elementary Psychology, or the First Principles of Mental and Moral Science for High, Normal and Other Secondary Schools and for Private Reading* by Daniel Putnam and *Rudimentary Psychology for Schools and Colleges* by G. M. Steele (Engle, 1967b).

FROM 1900 TO 1940

According to Engle (1967b), psychology was offered in high schools in Iowa (and probably other states as well) before and soon after the turn of the century as a "professional" course for students who intended to teach in the elementary grades after completion of high school. A semester or summer at a normal school was enough in those days to obtain a teaching license if a student had already had the professional psychology course as part of his or her high school training. "As early as 1910 psychology was in the curriculum of the Kansas City schools and ... by 1973 it was estimated that two thirds of the high schools in the state of Kansas offered psychology" (Engle, 1967b, p. 169). A 1937 APA committee report indicated that "from 1929 to 1934 there was a steady increase in the popularity of psychology courses in the high school curriculum" (quoted in Engle, 1967b, p. 169).

Early in the 1930s psychology was recognized by at least one author (Moore, 1932) as an appropriate topic already being taught as a unit in junior high school science. According to a doctoral dissertation at the time (Bronson, 1932; Pechstein & Bronson, 1933), about half of the state directors of secondary education sampled and a little more than half of 100 principals of high schools with enrollments of 1,000 or more either offered or favored offering psychology as a subject at the senior high school level. Favoring such offerings also were 53% of 90 presidents of teachers colleges and 60% of heads of departments of secondary education in 62 universities. A survey in 1933–34 by the U.S. Office of Education indicated that psychology courses were then being offered in some schools in at least 15 states (Noland, 1966a).

The second half of the 1930s yielded two lengthy reports (Stone & Watson, 1936, 1937) on the teaching of psychology in secondary schools, and there were a number of additional articles on the teaching of psychology in the high school and the grade school (e.g., Engle, 1939; Geisel, 1938; Harris, 1939; McCall, 1936, 1937; Riddle, 1939; Salisbury, 1936; Skaggs, 1937).

FROM 1940 TO 1960

During the first half of the 1940s, Ralph Ojemann began his work on helping youth learn about the causes of behavior (McNiel, 1944; Morgan & Ojemann, 1942). Further surveys, texts, and articles appeared, and an increased interest became evident in high school courses in mental hygiene (e.g., Geisel 1940, 1943a, 1943b; Turney & Collins, 1940). The first edition of T. L. Engle's influential, discipline-oriented text, *Psychology: Its Principles and Applications*, was published in 1945, and by the latter half of the 1940s Ralph Ojemann's approach, empirically demonstrating the effectiveness of teaching about the science of behavior to elementary pupils, was gathering further momentum (Ojemann, 1948, 1949; Ojemann, Nugent, & Corry, 1947).

Developments in the early 1950s indicated that the teaching of psychology in the high schools and mental health instruction in the elementary grades were coming of age (Elliott, 1950–51; Hertzman, 1952; Ojemann, 1953; Rosenthal, 1953). Roback (1952) published a historical article on psychology teaching in secondary schools, and Bunch (1954, 1955) prepared two lengthy reports for the APA. Engle (1950) wrote a review of 13 texts expressly intended for the high school level and undertook a series of surveys concerning the extent of the precollege endeavor, the preparation of high school psychology teachers, and the attitudes of teachers and students toward the high school psychology course (1951, 1952a, 1952b, 1952c, 1955). One survey at a California state teachers college revealed that almost 10% of students enrolled in a sophomore-level general psychology course had had a psychology course in high school (Burnett, 1952).

During the later 1950s, the growth that had marked the preceding years increased ever more rapidly and major concern began to be expressed about standards for teachers of high school psychology (Coffield, 1959; Crouter, 1956). There was a growing flurry of papers on high school psychology in general, and instruction that was partly mental health related and partly discipline oriented was working its way down into the middle grades, with an elementary psychology course taught at the eighth-grade level in this country (Patti, 1956). A fifth-grade program for personal development was described and evaluated by Solvertz and Lund in 1956; and in 1959 Ralph Ojemann published a book on his program for education in human behavior in the primary grades.

THE 1960s

Another history of the field, together with further national survey data showing that precollege psychology was continuing to grow rapidly, was published by Coffield and Engle in 1960. In the same year, Engle published two papers (1960a, 1960b) on the preparation of high school psychology teachers, and Snellgrove (1962) put together a mimeographed manual for high school psychology teachers on the construction and use of inexpensive psychological apparatus. During 1964 and 1965, under the auspices of APA's Division on the Teaching of Psychology, a mimeographed list of over 1,700 names and addresses of known high school psychology teachers was compiled, as were a dittoed list of some 40 psychology films, a recommended list of readings appropriate for the high school student, a catalog of companies that sold psychological apparatus, and a 16-page, partly annotated bibliography for high school psychology teachers and students. These materials were available free to any high school teacher of psychology.

Other avenues for the promotion and improvement of psychology in secondary schools were also explored, such as the encouragement of psychological entries in high school science fairs (Coffield, Engle, McNeely, & Milton, 1960) and the inclusion of psychology in a traveling science teacher program for high schools (Ratner, 1961). That the American Psychological Association was anxious to cooperate with high school psychology teachers was made clear in 1963, when its Division on the Teaching of Psychology invited high school teachers of psychology to become affiliates, to receive its newsletter, and to participate in psychology conventions.

State surveys of high school psychology teaching continued in the '60s (e.g., Anderson, 1965; McNeely, 1967; Noland, 1966b). Stanley and Abrams (1965) explored the question of the certification of psychology majors to teach in the high school, with a survey finding that the western states were more likely to hire such applicants than were other parts of the country. The mental health theme continued to be emphasized in high school psychology teaching (e.g., Belenky, 1966; Hollister, 1966) and was also flourishing at the elementary level (Burnes, 1966; Gertz, 1966; Roen, 1966; Sigel & Waters, 1966). Other efforts at the elementary and junior high levels included those of Lippitt et al. (1963), who prepared the rationale for what was soon to be their major curriculum project to teach behavioral science at the upper elementary and lower middle school levels, and Sheldon Roen (1965), who defended teaching of the behavioral sciences at the lower elementary grades. Klugh, Deterline, and Henderson (1960) described the teaching of Skinner's descriptive behaviorism in the fifth grade.

In 1967, Engle published a paper on the objectives for and the kinds of subject matter stressed in high school, offering quantitative evidence that high school teachers of psychology favored a personal-adjustment over a discipline orientation in psychology courses. A new note in the 1960s was the influence of far-reaching reforms in social science curricula, as major social science curriculum projects in geography and other fields reached fruition. A representative document that characterizes the new social science curricula is *Concepts and Structure in the New Social Science Curricula* (Morrissett, 1967).

A true landmark in the teaching of precollege psychology was the appearance in 1967 of an entire issue of the *Journal of School Psychology* devoted to this topic. The guest editor, Jack I. Bardon, gained the cooperation of most of the major figures in the area at the time as well as of several less well-known ones. Appropriately enough, the issue opened with an optimistic yet objective paper (Engle, 1967b) on the past, present, and possible future of the teaching of psychology at the secondary level. An article by Noland (1967) summarized the results of a survey of school psychologists and counselors. It was indicated that (a) over 90% of the respondents favored the teaching of psychology at the high school level; (b) the great majority preferred a "practical," personal-adjustment course or a combination of scientific and practical content, but 95% rejected an exclusively scientific treatment of psychology; and (c) almost three quarters favored mandatory state certification of high school psychology teachers.

Other papers in the issue covered topics as diverse as the notable increase in offerings of psychology as a separate course of instruction and recommendations on the preparation of elementary and high school teachers of psychology. Also included were papers covering elementary instruction in the causes of behavior and discussions of various ways in which psychology could be included in the curriculum. Concluding the issue was a valuable set of book reviews and a particularly useful bibliography of relevant literature on precollege psychology compiled by Noland and Bardon (1967).

RECENT TRENDS

Among the more influential events since 1967 has been the appearance of the semipopular monthly magazine, *Psychology Today*, which began in the spring of 1967. Many teachers of psychology have found this magazine, with its readable style, superb illustrations, and focus on "human" psychology, an interesting source for classroom materials. In 1972 the same publisher issued the second edition of a large, profusely illustrated introductory survey textbook, entitled *Psychology Today: An Introduction*, and an accompanying set of readings. This material has been used at the high school level as well as in colleges, which were its primary target audience.

Material for behavioral science teaching in grades three through seven was published by Science Research Associates in 1969 (Lippitt, Fox, & Schaible). This material was the product of a major curriculum development effort of the '60s. Focused primarily on social psychology, and based on the philosophy of an inquiry approach, the material is a fully developed package of innovative instructional units that use a modified laboratory strategy and involve students in gathering, organizing, and using data concerning human behavior.

Also in 1969, *Introduction to the Behavioral Sciences: An Inquiry Approach* (Sandberg, 1969) appeared. It was the final segment of the Holt Social Studies Curriculum, which is intended for use at the senior high school level. Its title describes the content of the textbook well. Beginning, like the Science Research Associates' materials, with a unit on the nature of behavioral science and the conduct of inquiry, it takes up several substantive areas of interest to the high school student, such as adolescence, the search for identity, and race and prejudice.

Also during 1969, the fifth edition of Engle's highly successful text (Engle, 1945) was published, with the coauthorship of Snellgrove. It was accompanied by a teacher's manual and a record of activities and experiments to use with the text. A sixth edition of the work (Engle & Snellgrove, 1974) is now available.

A number of other materials expressly designed for high schools have been published. A low-key, descriptive, nonpolemical, and traditionally oriented introductory text with a historical slant is out in a second edition (Branca, 1968). Gordon (1972) has prepared a text slanted toward clinical psychology, to the relative neglect of scientific, experimental parts of the field with a strong focus on topics of interest to high school students. In its third edition is the Sorenson, Malm, and Forehand (1971) text, which is at the humanistic extreme of the polarity we shall develop later in this document. Didactic in approach, and with no effort to present either an overview of contemporary psychology or the relevance of research results to real-life problems, it presents wisdom and advice about personality, interpersonal relations, and mental hygiene. The text of another curriculum package intended primarily for the high school psychology course was published in 1971 (Wertheimer, Björkman, Lundberg, & Magnusson, 1971). Its focus is an evidential approach to the study of behavior, combined with references to the applicability of a few broad psychological principles to everyday life. Although brief, it contains many recommended exercises, activities, experiments, and suggested further avenues of inquiry, and attempts to provide a representative overview of the discipline.

Since 1967, the American Psychological Association has also entered the field of high school psychology in a significant way. The APA participated in an interdisciplinary behavioral science conference in 1967 in Williamsburg, Virginia, funded by the National Science Foundation. An outcome of this conference was a recommendation that a curriculum for the teaching of behavioral science in general should be developed for the upper middle school and/or lower high school grades and that courses in the separate behavioral sciences (including anthropology, psychology, and sociology) should be developed for the upper high school grades. A growing number of symposia and programs on precollege psychology have been scheduled in recent years at national, regional, and state psychological association conventions.

In December 1969, with funds from the U.S. Office of Education, APA brought together a group of its ex-presidents who prepared a statement on "Psychology in the Educational Venture." It supported substantial involvement of APA and individual psychologists in the improvement of precollege instruction in psychology. In 1969, retiring APA president George A. Miller provided further impetus by devoting his presidential address to the theme of "giving psychology away" to those who can use it to improve their own lives, that is, as a means of promoting human welfare.

Early in 1970, additional funds were obtained from the U.S. Office of Education for an APA-sponsored five-week program on the teaching of psychology in the secondary school, at Oberlin College. In the months immediately preceding the program at Oberlin College, a Clearinghouse on Precollege Psychology and Behavioral Science was established by APA. Its first task was to gather support materials for the summer program, but a more long-range dissemination function was intended and subsequently realized. A landmark resource book for high school psychology teachers resulted from this conference (Bare et al., 1970); it is now available in a second edition (APA, 1973).

In late 1970, APA's Division on the Teaching of Psychology charged Raymond G. Hunt with the job of drafting a coordinated plan for development of precollege psychology that would bring together under one centralized administration a number of existing projects and some to be newly generated. Early in 1971, Hunt, Davol, and Schoeppe collected the contributions of a large number of people and fashioned "A Proposal for Precollege Psychology and Behavioral Science" (1972), a document that played a significant role in subsequent deliberations concerning the APA high school psychology curriculum development project.

Also in 1971, the United States Office of Education provided support for the development of two prototypic curriculum modules for the high school, one on reinforcement (Markman, 1973) and the other on race relations (Kasschau, 1974a). The development of these modules was seen by APA as part of the process of moving toward a massive curriculum development effort at the high school level. In the summer of 1972, John K. Bare of Carleton College was appointed director of a proposed secondary school curriculum development project in human behavior; and in February 1973 a proposal for the project was submitted over his signature to the National Science Foundation (NSF). The Human Behavior Curriculum Project (HBCP) was approved by NSF and began operation in January 1974. Under the guidance of a 15-member Steering Committee composed of educators experienced in curriculum development and prominent psychologists, including four former presidents of APA, HBCP is encouraging the development of 30 teaching modules, each sufficient for two weeks or so of classroom activities. Typically, a module is to be developed by a design team including a college-level psychologist, two high school teachers, and two high school students. The modules are to be extensively field tested in the project, which is expected to take five years for completion.

On other fronts, recent years have also seen the appearance of more periodic and separate publications concerned with the teaching of psychology. The newsletter of APA's Division (2) on the Teaching of Psychology began publishing a number of articles on the teaching of psychology in the schools in 1964. *Periodically*, a newsletter for high school teachers, has been issued monthly during the academic year since January 1971 by the APA Clearinghouse. In 1971 appeared the first issues of a commercially published semi-annual journal, *People Watching*, devoted primarily to the teaching of behavioral science in the elementary grades, but touching on high school behavioral science as well. The first issue of still another commercially published journal intended to serve high school and community college teachers of psychology, sociology, and anthropology, *The Behavioral and Social Science Teacher*, appeared in early 1974.

A major report on undergraduate education, providing the findings of a large-scale APA-sponsored project funded by NSF, has recently been published (Kulik, 1973). Many of the philosophical issues and questions of the how, why, when, and where of the teaching of psychology at the college level discussed in this book are also clearly relevant to precollege psychology. Accordingly, the contents of this volume are likely to be as interesting to psychology teachers in the schools as to psychology teachers in the colleges and universities.

Recently, the ERIC Clearinghouse for Social Studies/Social Science Education, with the cosponsorship of APA, commissioned two documents directly relevant to precollege psychology. The intent was to provide a package of items that would be useful to the field. The first is a booklet (Bare, 1971) designed to help the teacher who has just been handed the assignment of instituting a new psychology course. The second, the present document, is intended to provide the history and background of the teaching of psychology in the schools, to present the philosophical issues associated with such instruction, and to discuss recent trends in the field.

In sum, it is clear that various national institutions have finally recognized the existence of psychology teaching at the precollege level and are beginning to do something that will help in this endeavor.

SOME RECENT SURVEY RESULTS

Let us end this brief history by discussing a few recent findings from surveys that attest to the growth of the teaching of psychology, especially in the secondary schools, raise some problems, and characterize what is going on.

In 1951 only nine states certified high school psychology teachers, but by 1964, 26 states did so (Thornton & Colver, 1967), and now 37 states do (Johnson, 1973b). Typical high school teachers of psychology have had, over the years, only some eight or nine credit hours of courses in psychology departments (Abrams & Stanley, 1967; Engle, 1952c). Stahl and Casteel (1973) summarize the results of other surveys as follows:

Studies of secondary school psychology courses during the past two decades have tended to substantiate each other. The following list briefly summarizes the important characteristics and facts relative to the status of precollege psychology.
    1. Student enrollment and numbers of schools offering the course are rapidly increasing.
    2. Students and teachers see the course as being valuable.
    3. There is a [perceived] need for psychology courses in the curriculum.
    4. Courses are very popular among students.
    5. Courses are offered in all fifty states.

6. Courses are most often one semester in length.
7. Courses are offered as an elective more often than as a required subject.
8. Courses are more likely to be offered in schools with over 300 students.
9. Courses are most frequently opened to juniors and seniors.
10. Girls are more likely to take the course than boys.
11. Whites are more likely to enroll in the course than blacks.
12. The course is offered most often in urban school settings.
13. Personal adjustment and mental hygiene are the two most often stated objectives of the course.
14. Courses are usually assigned social studies credit.
15. Teachers are predominantly certified in social studies.
16. Teachers develop and use a great deal of materials such as popular magazines to supplement their courses.
17. The T. L. Engle and Louis Snellgrove textbook, *Psychology: Its Principles and Applications*, is the most popular text used.
18. Psychology is not required in any state for graduation.
19. More schools would offer the course if properly trained teachers were available. (pp. 27–28)

Some further statistics attest to the growth of psychology in the schools. In 1950 there were an estimated 1,080 public high schools offering a course in psychology (Engle, 1951); by 1960 the number had grown to 2,362 (Wright, 1965), and by 1970, to 5,779 (Gertler & Barker, 1972). Surveys by the National Science Teachers Association identified 5,645 high school psychology teachers in the fall of 1969; 6,689 in 1971; and 7,472 in 1973; taking account of nonrespondents in these surveys (24%, 22%, and 22%, respectively), these figures can be adjusted to approximately 7,400, 8,800, and 9,600. It therefore seems reasonable to estimate that there well may be considerably more than 10,000 high school psychology teachers in 1974.

Data from recent state surveys are typical of the many studies that have been undertaken. John Hampton (1973) reported that questionnaires were sent to 478 schools in Oklahoma; 209 (43%) returned them, yielding 112 high schools identified as currently having a psychology program.

The larger the school, the more likely it is that it will have a psychology program, as 100% of the schools with more than 1,000 students, 76% of the schools with between 400 and 1,000 students, and 54% of the schools with less than 400 students have such courses.

Moreover . . . most schools (87%) have only one teacher involved in teaching psychology. In general these teachers focused on psychology as an approach to life (83%) as opposed to psychology as a science (17%). Most teachers of psychology had some undergraduate education in psychology (more than 90%); however, less than half of them had any graduate preparation in psychology. (Hampton, 1973, p. 5)

Thornton and Williams (1971) summarize some slightly older data from Florida, as follows:

Presently enrolled in high school psychology courses in Florida are 400 tenth-grade students (representing ¼ of 1% of the total number of students enrolled in the tenth grade in Florida), 1,800 eleventh-grade students (representing 1½% of the total number of students enrolled in the eleventh grade in Florida), and 14,000 twelfth-grade students (representing 15% of the total number of students enrolled in the twelfth grade in Florida). (p. 1040)

They then compare
the growth of two other "New Social Studies" in Florida's high schools with that of the growth of psychology.... Presently enrolled in high school sociology courses in Florida are 208 tenth-grade students (representing ⅛ of 1% of the total number of students enrolled in the tenth grade in Florida), 1,000 eleventh-grade students (representing %₀ of 1% of the total number of students enrolled in the eleventh grade in Florida) and 10,000 twelfth-grade students (representing 12% of the total number of students enrolled in the twelfth grade in Florida schools). (p. 1040)

As for a separate course in political science, it is not offered in the tenth grade in Florida, and only 350 (one third of 1%) eleventh graders and 306 (one third of 1%) twelfth graders were enrolled in such a course at the time.

Of course, it must be recognized that these figures were obtained just before major new curriculum packages became available in sociology and political science; the picture may be different now. Making such cross-discipline comparisons is difficult, especially given the likelihood of different definitions of what constitutes a "psychology" and "sociology" course in different states. However, Gertler and Barker (1972), summarizing the results of a national survey and comparing enrollment by disciplines in 1960–61 and 1970–71, report that enrollment in sociology jumped from 2.5 to 4.3% of the total national enrollment while enrollment in psychology jumped from 1.2 to 2.8%, indicating a faster rate of growth in psychology enrollments over the decade. The relative popularity of precollege psychology has been documented in a variety of other states including South Carolina, where statewide enrollment figures have shown psychology to be the most popular elective social studies course offered at the high school level in 1971, 1972, and 1973 (Kasschau & Michael, 1973).

Thornton and Williams (1971) end their article with the following comments, the last two sentences of which still stand in spite of our qualifications:

Obviously, these "New Social Studies" offerings have not proven to be nearly as popular and pervasive as high school psychology.... It is imperative that we have professionally trained teachers in psychology if students are to achieve maximum benefits from this area of the high school curriculum. Psychology is too important a field of study to be taught by unqualified and uncertified teachers. (p. 1040)

In the context of the figures just cited, the question raised by many about why psychology should even be included in precollege curricula is rendered functionally moot. The more appropriate concern should be how best to offer the course. It is this latter concern that serves as our focal point.

Philosophy

Accompanying the growth in psychology course enrollments in high schools (and in colleges) has been a debate concerning course content and the most effective techniques to be used in communicating that content. It is a debate based in the discipline itself, reflecting a clash between two fundamentally different philosophies.

What should be the goal of precollege psychology courses? The disagreement over goals is reflected in the following:

What and how to teach psychology brought the group into sharp disagreement. Two opposing sides were immediately established. One proposed that a) all textbooks on the high school level be eliminated and b) that we encourage open dialogue in the effort to get at self knowledge, as well as at the personal and social problems of each student. The other side proposed that we transmit a body of scientific knowledge. (Merrifield & Schoeppe, 1969, p. 39)

In general, however, there exists relative consistency of views that high school courses should be personal-social adjustment oriented rather than presented as an empirical science. (Noland, 1967, pp. 119; 181)

An understanding of social processes gained by using analytical tools correctly will develop children's problem-solving ability, a quality which is a necessary prerequisite of good citizenship in a free society. . . . We have taken the approach of using the individual structures of the disciplines as a basis for the social science curriculum from grade one through grade twelve. (Senesh, pp. 126, 127, quoted in Morrissett & Stevens, 1971)

Such disagreement is healthy, but an understanding of the central issue is critical to any decision about curriculum, teaching methods, and course goals. Providing a balanced overview of psychology as a scientific discipline, helping students see the relevance of psychological knowledge to their own lives and assisting students in articulating their own feelings and patterns of social interaction are all potentially legitimate goals and, while somewhat interrelated, also clearly distinct from each other.

THE CONTEXT

Let us begin by concentrating on the nature of the student population at issue. Recently, the Commissioner of High Education in South Carolina (J. A. Morris, personal communication, November 1972) developed some interesting statistics concerning the various points at which students exit from the system of public education. Talking specifically about South Carolina, but using statistics that are presumably generalizable, he noted that of 100 students entering the first grade only 50 remain to graduate from high school. Of those who graduate, approximately one third (16 or so) go on to some form of advanced education, but of that number only about half choose a college or university education. In other words, eight of every 100 youngsters entering elementary school reach a college or university. Although the absolute numbers may well vary from state to state, there are at least two points to be noted.

First, constantly improving educational techniques (new curricula, audiovisual technology, etc.), the increasing emphasis that our society places on the high school diploma, and the many changes being wrought by busing and desegregation have introduced within the system of public education what Klingelhofer (1972) calls "The New Student." This student is sometimes condescendingly described as disadvantaged, culturally different, or high risk, but is typified by blacks, Indians, Puerto Ricans, Mexican-Americans, and the like. In other words, the diversity and complexity of the consumers of public education are increasing. It can be argued that as student diversity increases, the means of meeting students' needs should likewise increasingly diversify.

Second, the complexity and diversity of students' goals make it necessary to ask how psychology is to meet these and society's too. The number of potential goals is great indeed: a good job, knowledge of the discipline, an improved life, good citizenship, self-understanding, "how to win friends and influence people," and so on. But from a practical point of view, students in psychology courses in elementary and secondary schools can be divided into two categories: those who will and those who will not ultimately go on to college. There is a substantial issue here as to whether those who are likely to have additional exposure to formal instruction in psychology at a later time in their life should be treated any differently in a precollege psychology course than those who are not (Kasschau, 1974b).

Undergraduate institutions, too, have been grappling for some time with the problems of how to deal with student demands, and numerous solutions to the problems have been developed. These include advanced placement examinations and challenge systems, courses for majors and nonmajors, and approaches to introductory psychology almost as broad as the number of institutions themselves.

> Graduate school orientations are often considered inappropriate in the undergraduate curriculum in psychology, and indeed a curriculum exclusively oriented toward graduate work would not meet the needs of most students in psychology courses. (Kulik, 1973, p. 202)

Similarly, exclusive orientation of high school psychology courses to college-preparatory students would clearly not meet the needs of many students enrolled.

The diversity of student goals and future educational opportunities and the diversity of options available in higher education justify the position that psychology courses in the high school should proceed independently of college-level demands. A substantial majority of precollege psychology students will have no further formal exposure to psychology.

This fact argues for a concentration on more pragmatic aspects of the discipline, emphasizing its applications—and the limits of such applications. But even so general a goal as this would appear somewhat oversimplified and not totally self-evident. It is also not immediately obvious what kind of course design would achieve this objective.

With these several perspectives in mind (student diversity, the variety of needs, the probability that many high school psychology courses are likely to be the last institutionalized contact between the discipline and the student), let us consider possible goals for precollege psychology courses.

GOALS

Walker and McKeachie (1967), in a useful book concerning the issues and techniques of teaching the college-level introductory course in psychology, discuss a series of goals that apply equally well to the precollege level. They mention (p. 13) the following goals: communicate elementary concepts; communicate facts; introduce the student to the full range of subject matter; integrate course material; communicate basic attitudes of the discipline; communicate the intrinsic interest of the subject matter; present the newest developments in the field; provide individual guidance and monitoring; develop selected intellectual skills; provide a suitable identification model for the student.

A high school teacher with a slightly different, more directly pragmatic, interest desires that her students:

know the body of psychological knowledge, recognize the names of those who have contributed to it, be skeptical, demand evidence for the statements about behavior, find flaws in such statements, be aware of the tentativeness of scientific findings, and be able to read critically articles about psychology. (Miller, 1972, p. 83)

Such ideas are consistent with one set of goals for the high school psychology course, the discipline-centered, "natural science" approach.

However, school psychologists, for example, tend to support another set of goals for such a course—goals more concerned with personal adjustment and development. At least 50% of a sample of these professionals endorsed each of the following (Noland, 1967, p. 180) as appropriate objectives for such a course: (a) should result in better knowledge, understanding, and acceptance of self on the part of the student; (b) the limitations as well as the sound uses of psychology in the resolution of personal-social problems should be stressed; (c) problems of personal adjustment should be stressed so that the pupil will better understand himself, now and in the future; (d) should emphasize family relationships and adjustment; (e) should provide assistance in handling emerging problems of boy-girl relationships; (f) should emphasize the values and limitations of emotional experiences; (g) should present sound psychological materials and principles but with major emphasis on those topics which are most practical and enjoyable; (h) should emphasize personality and character formation; (i) should help prepare students for future single or married roles; (j) should be of practical value to the school dropout; and (k) a major objective should be provision for sound educational and occupational planning and guidance.

There is, clearly, a fundamental difference—indeed, almost an incompatibility—between these two sets of goals. For some educators, the primary aim is to convey the facts and methods of the discipline; for others, the discipline in service of the self, both internally and socially, should be the focus. Some prefer "process," and others, "content." This basic disagreement makes it impossible to specify a single universally acceptable set of goals for precollege psychology instruction. Yet the teacher cannot avoid coming to grips with this question; upon the resolution of it depend not only the broad outlines of the course but also the details of day-to-day class assignments and interactions. As Walker and McKeachie (1967) put it, "What is really important is that the instructor formulate a set of goals or objectives he wishes to meet" (p. 11). After such objectives have been specified, and *only* after they have been specified, does it make sense to begin to design the course.

ISSUES

The 1973 Kasschau and Michael survey of high school psychology teachers in South Carolina included a question regarding the "slant" or emphasis of the local psychology course. Of the 84 teachers identifying a single slant, 42% indicated they taught their course as a "behavioral science," 27% indicated "personal adjustment," 18% indicated "social science," and the remaining 13% had a variety of not clearly identifiable orientations. Another 29 teachers (for a total of 113 of 226 potential respondents) indicated more than one slant or emphasis for their course. Interestingly, 96% of all respondents indicated that psychology is contained within the social science or social studies department of their school, and the remaining 4% represented teachers of only one psychology course whose primary department was not in sciences at all. Not a single teacher indicated he or she reported to a physical or natural science department.

The social science-natural science issue that college-level psychologists debate is, then, apparently not a source of contention in the high school. Many explanations suggest themselves, but prime among them is that teachers who are asked to teach psychology courses in high school usually have only minimal backgrounds in psychology. Further, in all likelihood, the psychology courses that they have taken have not emphasized the natural science aspects of the field. Laboratory equipment is not widely available for high school psychology courses.

At the level of "who reports to what department," the social science–natural science issue may seem to be easily resolved. But not so on a more philosophical level. The issue is firmly drawn in the first quotation in this section, selected from the report of a 1969 "Psychology for Youth Conference for High School Teachers of Psychology." At one point during the two-day conference the participants were subdivided into three small discussion groups. Group A reported:

> A discussion of teaching methods produced a definitely skewed distribution: most favored a nondirective, humanistic, experiential approach, but a preference was also expressed for a behavioristic administration with the teacher implementing the Skinnerian model by shaping the reactions of class members. (Merrifield & Schoeppe, 1969, p. 37)

Group B reported:

> The most important discussion, and that which took a great deal of the time of the group, was regarding the content of the course. A dichotomy arises between:
> a. an academic type course content, including a structured course, lecture type approach, using a textbook, and
> b. a dynamic interpersonal, experience type course, designed to help the student adjust, understand and cope with the environment—whatever that may encompass.
>
> There was disagreement as to whether some basic principles should be taught, and how they should be taught. (Merrifield & Schoeppe, 1969, p. 37)

Group C reported:

> What and how to teach psychology brought the group into sharp disagreement. Two opposing sides were immediately established. One proposed that a) all textbooks on the high school level be eliminated and b) that we encourage open dialogue in the effort to get at self knowledge, as well as at the personal and social problems of each student. The other side proposed that we transmit a body of scientific knowledge. (Merrifield & Schoeppe, 1969, p. 39)

In a very real sense all other issues are merely variations on this theme, cogently summarized by Bare (1971):

> Shall what is taught be knowledge of self or knowledge of others, principles or applications to personal and social problems, precision or significance, hard or soft? Viewing the issue as knowledge of self or knowledge of others, one sees a problem unique to psychology: the subject matter is both objective and subjective, and the explanations for phenomena must be satisfying not only scientifically but experientially. Psychology has been trying to bridge these poles since its inception. The study of consciousness was the study of me with the hope of understanding you; the study of behavior is the study of you with the hope of understanding me. (pp. 5 and 6)

The issue is an omnipresent one in both the history of psychology and in many contemporary meetings of teachers and researchers of things psychological. It is a debate that has many features and will doubtless never be fully resolved to everyone's satisfaction. In addition to being a debate between fundamentally different outlooks, between two alternative approaches to the discipline of psychology, between search and research, it is also a confrontation on two levels. It is on the one hand a debate of theorists, matching a Skinner or a Bruner against a Kohlberg or a Maslow, and on the other hand, an argument among practitioners, matching "personal adjusters" against the "guardians of the discipline."

It is theory at the abstract level and teaching technique at the pragmatic level. With these points in mind, let us address the issue by considering two major approaches that have been taken to teaching psychology at the precollege level—a personal-development orientation and a focus on the teaching of psychology as an academic discipline. Following discussion of these two approaches, the authors will propose a synthesis combining some of the best features of the more common views of the two.

PERSONAL DEVELOPMENT

If we have a discussion, how will we know when we get the right answer? —Anonymous

Why. A justification for the experiential, personal-development approach to psychology education is presented by Combs (1967) in a paper entitled "Humanizing Education: The Person in the Process." Combs expresses the view that American educators have become too enamored of the power of information, too enamored of facts, not enough concerned with students' abilities to use those facts to enhance their own lives, and not enough concerned with the students' feelings rather than their intellects. The student in the traditional school may get the impression that details are what is important; such an impression is apt to be fostered by multiple-choice or fill-in-the-blank examinations. Tests tend to be geared to what students do *not* know, probing for ever more specific facts, designed to produce a normal curve of grades. Combs decries the emphasis on machine-like memorization, writing that

> One of the things we Americans have learned to do better than anyone else in the world is to see the good life by letting the machines do what they do so well, thus setting us free to move in our own unique directions. In time we shall learn how to use our new hardware and I believe the machines will then increase our humanism. Meanwhile, we ought not to compete with the computers or make computers out of students. What is needed is to stress the qualities that make us unique, our humanity. (1967, p. 2)

Combs is expressing a more widely shared concern that education is aimed too much at fostering cognitive development and is neglecting, ignoring, or sacrificing affective development. The concern is sometimes phrased as "leaving the person out of the process." What the proponents of such arguments would like to substitute by way of specific goals is typically somewhat vague and therefore hard to develop since emphasis on process rather than content tends to be viewed as an end in itself. However, justifications for such aims usually cite one or more of the following kinds of goals:

1. "To teach growing children about their development in the context of their environment" (Roen, 1967, p. 205). Specifically, elementary school children should be taught basic social interpersonal skills, which are at least as useful as language and math.

2. To direct education toward the examination and understanding of growth experiences. Children, as they mature through adolescence into adulthood, are experiencing physical, emotional, and social changes at a rate not clearly related to their emerging ability to understand those changes. Education is the vehicle for diminishing the gap between experienced change and the ability to understand it.

3. To teach the social skills necessary to retain and perform a job. As students leave high school, whether by socially sanctioned graduation or by early withdrawal, many are faced with the prospect of assuming responsibility for supporting themselves. Education concerning the complex demands of the adult world, especially in the realm of interpersonal relations, should properly be the focus of psychology.

4. To facilitate the understanding of personal experiences and needs and develop a more serious appreciation of how to promote effective interpersonal interactions.

Collectively these goals provide justification for a person-oriented, experiential psychological education that emphasizes mental hygiene, personal growth, and self-understanding. In essence, the primary focus of this kind of education is the internal, subjective feelings and experiences of the student. The technique may vary, but to use Bare's (1971) language, it is essentially the study of me in an attempt to understand me (and maybe you).

Theory and technique. What are the theoretical underpinnings of this approach? The theories to be reviewed here, and in parallel discussions following, have in common a more or less specific applicability to the developing human from birth to adulthood. Any educator might read these discussions and feel comfortable that his or her students are being described. To that extent there is nothing in what follows that is of unique interest to teachers of psychology. Yet, when couched in terms of students' personal adjustment and hopes of improving it, these discussions take on special significance for teachers of psychology who endorse personal adjustment as the appropriate focus for precollege psychology. The theories yield a rationale for providing students with specific types of experiences depending on their developmental state and degree of wisdom.

It should be noted here, in anticipation of an issue equally applicable to this as to subsequent discussions on theory and techniques, that it is doubtful that conscious theoretical considerations underlie many of the approaches to teaching psychology discussed in this document. Certainly such theories do not undergird any one approach to the exclusion of alternate approaches nor are they offered solely as support of the approach being discussed. It is perhaps better to view the theories discussed in these sections as a matter of preference, not mandate.

Although aspects of the personal-adjustment form of psychological education can be traced back to the writings of Freud and even earlier, the primary theoretical positions supporting such efforts are drawn from formulations of the past 30 years. Among the theories that have been cited in support of this approach are ones that concern themselves with cognitive, moral, and social development.

Jean Piaget's theory of cognitive development has been a dominant factor for several decades. Piaget's is a theory that postulates that people progress through four uniquely identifiable stages in cognitive ability as they mature into adulthood (Inhelder & Piaget, 1958; Piaget, 1952).

Because Piaget's is a stage theory tied to the highly variable and interwoven processes of development, it emphasizes sequence, not the absolute time, of occurrence. The main thesis is that the developmental processes and the abilities that accompany them occur in some specifiable order. However, there is tentative evidence (e.g., Bryant & Trabasso, 1971) that Piagetian theorists may be in error with regard both to the age at which and even the order in which cognitive events occur. Whatever the eventual fate of this theory, it alerts curriculum developers to the need for specific training procedures—procedures that take student cognitive capabilities into account to achieve intended effects.

Lawrence Kohlberg's (1969) is also a theory of stages, but of stages in moral or ethical development rather than general cognitive processes. While the stages are not so tightly linked to specific chronological age as in Piaget's case, the assumption is that development of moral perspective proceeds through as many as six stages during the course of a person's life (although some of the latter stages may never be achieved by a mature adult).

Another significant approach is Erik Erikson's (1950) psychosocial theory of development, which closely parallels the first four of the five stages in personality development postulated by Freud. Erikson, however, modifies Freud's theory by expanding the final phase of development into four additional stages covering puberty and adolescence, young adulthood, adulthood, and maturity. Each of these stages is accompanied by a crisis, but as each crisis is adequately handled, the personality acquires another fundamental characteristic. For the adolescent the crisis is identity versus role confusion; resolution of that crisis as the individual moves into young adulthood determines whether an adequate identity will develop.

Abraham Maslow and Carl Rogers are two other humanistically oriented theorists whose views have received widespread recent attention. Both analyze and advocate the idea of *self-actualization,* the making actual of human potentials and possibilities for authentic selfhood, for productive, creative endeavor, and for effective, sincere, positive human interaction—potentials and possibilities that all too few people manage to realize. While neither Maslow's nor Rogers' theories have as yet been stated unequivocally enough to lead to concrete educational practices, many people have been inspired by their writings to strive for educational goals consistent with the maximum realization of human potential. Such high ideals are at least implicit in the thinking of those who advocate humanistic goals for precollege psychology.

From the abstraction of theory to the pragmatics of education is a rather substantial step. Let us consider specifically the high school senior, the student most likely to be enrolled in a psychology course at the secondary level. The lessons drawn here may generalize in process, but perhaps less so in content, to elementary or junior high school students. According to Piaget, a 16-year-old is capable of abstract consideration of the present and the future and of beliefs and values without egocentricity, a capacity that his or her preadolescent sibling does not have. In Kohlberg's (1969) system, this 16-year-old is fully capable of functioning and reasoning in terms of society's needs rather than solely his or her own needs. According to Erikson, this same 16-year-old is facing the crisis of identity formation; and for Maslow and Rogers, self-actualization is the major objective of "sweet sixteen." From an educator's perspective this stage must, then, be viewed as one potentially very rich in opportunity.

The approach to psychological education espoused by Mosher and Sprinthall (1970) is formulated in terms of this opportunity. It is an attempt to take advantage of a critical developmental stage to provide personally meaningful experiences in the affective as well as the purely cognitive domain, with the expectation of fostering optimal personal development (cf. Sprinthall, 1971). Combs (1967) has noted that

Psychologically, emotion is understood as an indicator of personal involvement. Things which have no personal meaning arouse no emotion. Things I care about I get emotional about. . . . Emotion is a question of personal involvement, an indicator of the degree to which ideas are likely to affect behavior. (p. 1)

Related to this, Sprinthall (1971) comments on the effective utilization of emotions in educational processes:

As Jones (1968) correctly noted, uncontrollable feelings and emotions can obstruct learning. But Jones is not advocating uncontrolled emotion as personal (psychological) education: he is suggesting very pointedly that children learn about their emotions in order to control them. Instead of answering the expression of emotion in school with silence, thus teaching the child to keep things to himself, Jones comments that emotion and feeling have a legitimate place in school particularly because "A child cannot . . . learn to share and use what he has not learned to control."

Even if we can accept the idea that emotion has a place in school, the essential educational problem remains: it is . . . difficult to specify affective/personal objectives. (p. 375)

The way in which this kind of theory is converted into actual educational curriculum is detailed in Mosher and Sprinthall's (1971) description of their well-developed high school psychology program. (See pp. 15–27 of their work for a fuller description.)

Other contributions that illustrate various approaches to psychological education with an emphasis on the improvement of mental health are the works of Roen and of Long in the elementary school and of Belenky in the high school. For a number of years, Roen has been advocating the teaching of behavioral sciences in elementary grades. He cites a number of benefits accruing from such efforts, most central of which is a broad social benefit:

From the point of view of mental health and social well-being, faith that knowledge will have its own rewards compels the assumption that avenues of primary prevention can be opened in the classroom setting. . . . On the level of secondary prevention, it can be argued that cognitive attention to problems experienced by children can influence their resolution. (1967, p. 206)

Far beyond advocating, Long (1971, 1971–72) has been implementing a behavioral science curriculum at the elementary level for several years, getting children to observe each other and themselves, to talk freely and openly about their feelings, and to engage in experiments and simulation games that provide them with additional perspectives on human behavior and interpersonal interaction. Long is convinced that the insights and positive self-regard that presumably result from such experiences can serve as a useful agent for primary prevention of mental disturbance and for the enhancement of mental health.

Mosher and Sprinthall, Roen, and Long provide reasoned support for the introduction of mental health and self-awareness concepts into public education at both the elementary and the secondary level. Belenky (1966) further advocates such an approach. He argues that secondary school counselors who deal with students' personal problems are self-limited in that role: their techniques are entirely verbal, and they refuse to recognize the effect they do have on their students. Belenky goes on to suggest that such counselors could increase their effectiveness if they would acknowledge their impact and more openly be willing to teach psychology courses.

The proposal is not a new one. Jersild and Helfant (1953) advocated a concept similar in impact, if not specific details, more than a decade earlier, and more recently Pietrofesa (1968, 1969) and Rappaport and Sorensen (1971) have offered similar arguments. All of these professionals want to use psychology in precollege curricula to facilitate personal adjustment and improve mental health.

The advocates say. Advocacy of teaching psychology to encourage students' personal development is strong, but so far this approach is only minimally supported by data. Sprinthall (1971) has noted the difficulty of specifying affective/personal objectives, and with that is inherited the problem of impartial assessment. Nevertheless, supporters include teachers, students, and a broader group of professionals. Teachers endorse "psychological education" for several reasons: (a) it offers a vehicle for teaching the principles of psychology while simultaneously fostering the personal development of students; (b) it decreases the perceived gap between the abstractions of an academic discipline and the real-life problems of maturing (pre-) adolescents; and (c) it typically encourages student involvement in role playing, in discussion, and in counseling situations with fellow students, all focused on their personal development, and, in so doing, it is seemingly quite effective in maintaining student interest in the subject.

Students favor teaching psychology to foster personal adjustment/development for similar reasons: (a) it addresses topics of immediate relevance to students, ranging from maturation-related problems to communication with peers and parent-child relations, all set in a context of the students' evolving personal development; (b) it is interesting and offers students the opportunity to view their peers in typically more relaxed, informal settings than are usually found in a school classroom; and (c) it often creates opportunities for students to engage in peer and cross-age teaching, the latter being an activity of special interest. In sum, from the students' perspective, "psychological education" addresses a topic of direct and personal concern, frequently offering a variety of teaching exercises that are highly effective in maintaining interest.

The broader group of professionals who advocate this approach to the teaching of psychology, although difficult to identify, includes school psychologists, guidance counselors, and some clinically oriented psychologists. Professionally, this group benefits in a variety of ways from "psychological education." It offers a means for detecting some of the students experiencing personal adjustment and/or developmental problems who should be referred to a school or clinical psychologist for more formalized counseling and/or therapy. The technique increases student appreciation for the services offered by clinical and school psychologists through the school's administrative facilities. In addition, from the perspective of preventive therapy, teaching psychology in this manner endeavors to offer the benefit of facilitating personal development.

A lengthy statement endorsing the use of "psychological education" was shaped under the guest editorship of Ivey and Alschuler in the May 1973 issue of the *Personnel and Guidance Journal*. Grouping articles into sections addressing conceptual models, techniques, programmatic approaches, and social applications more or less tangentially related, the issue focuses on the role of the counselor in "psychological education"; however, broader philosophical and educational issues are also addressed.

The critics reply. The critics of the personal-development, mental-health-oriented approach to psychological education raise a number of issues, many of which, paradoxically, help to explain its current popularity. Ross (1972) offers a particularly cogent analysis by conjecturing that, if asked to characterize contemporary psychology, a randomly selected member of the general public would likely say that it is concerned primarily with the mind, mental illness, Freud, and ESP, among other things. Secondary school students as well as teachers with little or no background in psychology may well hold the same beliefs. Two circumstances support the maintenance of those beliefs by teachers, according to Ross. First, the high school psychology teacher is isolated from the subject-matter specialists in colleges and universities. Second, it is a rare teacher who teaches only psychology, and even more rare is the one who has a colleague teaching psychology in the same school. Thus, unlike the college course taught by a trained professional to large, standardized, impersonal classes, the psychology course of the isolated local high school teacher is typically a small, nonstandardized, personal class in which student opinion, as mentioned earlier, carries markedly greater impact. The result may be a superficial concern for "relevance" and personal adjustment with little or no support for a discipline-oriented, let alone a discipline-based, psychology course.

The primary dangers the critics see coming from more humanistic, informal approaches to the discipline are the use of social science jargon and loose formulations without doing justice to the rigor of the discipline. They stress that adequate, successful use of individual growth-oriented psychological education looks easy but requires even harder work in preparation and use than a more solidly discipline-based course.

Critics also point to the problem of potential role conflict between the school psychologist and the school teacher of psychology. Williams (1972) specifically encourages such role conflict. He suggests that any teacher or school staff member could act as a consultant, that is, one who "tries to help the consultee utilize his own resources to deal effectively with whatever problems confront him" (p. 16). Belenky (1966), too, leans in this direction. He recommends that school counselors actively attempt to offer psychology courses as a means for changing behavior and increasing the self-understanding of students. Critics argue that a very fine line is being drawn—or blurred—here between the roles and responsibilities of a teacher and those of a school psychologist.

Another point raised by critics was represented in a previously cited study (Noland, 1967) of the appropriate content objectives for a high school psychology course. In that study, less than three in 10 school psychologists and counselors in Ohio would endorse designing the course primarily for the collegebound student or presenting a picture of scientific psychology in much the same way that chemistry and biology, among others, are presented. Moreover, when asked to rank-order guidance counselors, school psychologists, science teachers, and social studies teachers regarding the one currently best prepared to teach psychology, the school psychologists and counselors almost completely ignored the latter two groups and chose the school psychologist by a two-to-one margin over the guidance counselor. The same group did endorse more university training by department of psychology faculty for prospective psychology teachers, but 95% rejected the offering of an exclusively scientific psychology course. Critics of the "personal development" focus can argue that students in such courses are being done a disservice because they are being taught misconceptions of what psychology is "really" about.

In substance, the latter two issues above relate to the appropriateness of school psychologists and guidance counselors as teachers of psychology. Concern is being expressed about their apparently rather strongly "antiscientific" bias and about the dangers of mixing professional guidance and counseling problems with the teaching of psychology in the schools. These are, in a sense, criticisms based on defense of the disciplinarian approach rather than specific opposition to the goals of personal adjustment and mental health.

Still another criticism directed toward "psychological education" concerns the very inadequate data regarding the validity and stability of the presumed educational goals achieved by this technique. Sprinthall (1971), for one, has anticipated this criticism by noting the difficulty of specifying affective/personal educational objectives. With that difficulty comes the problem, and hence the concern, regarding impartial assessment. In addition to the difficulty of demonstrating that the experiential forms of teaching do indeed lead to the desired outcomes, there is also, finally, the nagging worry that such techniques, especially in the hands of teachers who are not thoroughly trained in orthopsychiatry, clinical psychology, or psychiatry, may actually produce more psychological harm than benefit to the students.

PSYCHOLOGY AS A DISCIPLINE

*Any subject can be taught
effectively in some intellectually
honest form to any child at any
stage of development.*
—J. S. Bruner

Why. At the opposite pole from the mental-health/psychological growth perspective is the aim of teaching psychology as a legitimate scientific discipline in its own right. Essentially a return to the discipline itself, it is typified by McKeachie (1962). McKeachie acknowledges that psychology contains some knowledge that could facilitate personal development and self-understanding (i.e., enhance subjective happiness, productivity, and social effectiveness); nevertheless, he makes clear his feeling that adjustment per se should not be a major goal of psychological instruction.

Variations on this basic sentiment are the touchstone of those who advocate the teaching of psychology in terms of its basic principles, concepts, and terms, rather than the application of psychology in the interests of personal adjustment and self-understanding. Among the common themes underlying advocacy of the disciplinary approach to education are the following:

1. Self-understanding is an admirable goal, but the most effective route to its achievement is through initial understanding of the discipline in terms of which investigation of self can be conducted. The cardinal

principles of psychology are few enough, and the complexity of self is great enough, that a rationally organized, disciplinary approach is the more fruitful means to achieve self-understanding.

2. Ours is, at heart, a knowledge-based, rational society. Moreover, the rate of increase in the generation of knowledge is itself increasing. It is best to start with knowledge itself, not subjective individual experience, and use that knowledge as the basis for teaching how to process and apply knowledge. It has been noted,

We are training children for an age which we don't even foresee. We are giving the children knowledge that we want them to use in the 21st century. A hundred years ago the idea that our children are a generation ahead was a platitude. Today it is a drama. No longer can parents understand their children when they come home from modern mathematics or modern science classes. The stage where parents will not understand their children when they talk about the nature of society will soon be reached. (Senesh, 1973)

The features of present society most likely to be present in future society are the basic, organizing principles of our disciplines. The facts will change and are too numerous to be learned, but the underlying assumptions, the methods, the basic theorems and laws organizing the facts of a discipline are much more stable (cf. Kuhn, 1970).

3. Psychology is still a relatively young discipline. It is concerned with the study of human (and animal) behavior; yet its organizing principles are few, and its explanatory laws are limited in scope. It is impossible to justify an examination of the detailed, complex processes of self directly with any hope of other than shallow, superficial explanation. Furthermore, direct ruminations about self, unaided by the body of psychological knowledge that does exist, are unlikely to be very fruitful.

4. Ultimately, the progress of a science is based on the research of its artisans, its scientists. With few exceptions, the major revisions of scientific theory and the signal discoveries are generated in a laboratory-based environment rather than in the armchair or the relatively uninformed discussion group.

These are some of the philosophical statements behind the disciplinarians' argument for teaching psychology in terms of the principles, methods, and generalities of the science, rather than the vagaries of the self. At least two other sources of support can be cited for this approach to education in psychology, based at least partly on the considerations just listed, but also representing "the spirit of the times."

First, as was mentioned earlier, George Miller (1969) in his presidential address to the American Psychological Association at the close of the '60s, presented a far-ranging perspective that listed some of the ills in contemporary society, noted the broad range of phenomena that psychologists are currently investigating, and lamented the "play-it-close-to-the-chest" attitude of many psychologists—the unwillingness to maintain contact with the society that supports so many of their investigations. Miller asserted that the noblest effort of psychologists in the current era of social turmoil would be to "give psychology away," that is, to package and translate it into such a form that it could be used by society. Not an advocacy of abandoning research, Miller's was rather a plea for communicating the findings of research to the general public. For precollege courses in psychology, this plea implies the presentation of the principles of psychology and their careful, considered application to everyday problems.

Second, T. L. Engle, unquestionably the dean of high school psychology, cites as one of the prime justifications for teaching psychology in the secondary schools the increased appreciation for "the ways in which the general methods of science can be applied to problems of behavior" (1969, p. vi). Combined with the recent address of Miller, Engle's position represents a firm source of continuing support for education in psychology from the disciplinary perspective. And few would deny that the discipline of psychology does have a great deal to offer to the understanding of behavior. In terms of the analysis offered by Bare (1971), this represents the study of you (collectively) in the interest of understanding you (and me).

Theory and technique. Basically, the disciplinarians argue that psychology has matured sufficiently to be taught in its own right to people who want to find out about it. There is no more need for a theoretical justification for teaching psychology than there is a need for a theoretical justification for teaching astronomy, or physics, or biology. The modern citizen should be as well informed about psychology as about other areas of human knowledge. Unfortunately, the distinction between the personal-adjustment educators and the disciplinarians—or more broadly the distinction between those advocating education for knowledge of self and those advocating education for knowledge of others—represents a split between university-level psychologists and those involved in precollege education. We have had occasion to raise this point before. It is well illustrated by the results of a survey reported by Engle (1967a), who asked 257 high school teachers of psychology, "What is the basic orientation for your course in psychology: considered to be part of the Science curriculum, considered to be part of the Social Studies curriculum?" Of 130 high school teachers responding, only 14 (11%) indicated the course was considered part of the science curriculum, while 109 (84%) indicated social studies, and seven (5%) indicated it was part of the general curriculum. By contrast, of 40 psychologists in higher education polled, 18 of the 31 replying (58%) believed the course should be part of the science curriculum, 12 (39%) indicated social studies, and only one (3%) would offer it as a general credit course.

Similarly, when asked to rank order seven objectives for the high school psychology course, these two groups of people responded as indicated in Table 1. The greatest difference of opinion involves the objective of developing an understanding of and appreciation for the uniqueness of the individual student and the application of psychological principles to the solution of personal problems. This was the first priority objective of the high school teachers, but only the fourth priority objective of the psychologists. On the other hand, the objective of developing an appreciation for psychology as a field of scientific knowledge—including developing a fundamental technical vocabulary and familiarity with basic research methods and stimulating curiosity concerning problems of behavior—was ranked first by the psychologists. The teachers, despite considerable disagreement about the precise rank, nevertheless, typically ranked it much lower.

TABLE 1   Mean Ranks Given Seven Course Objectives by 130 High School Teachers and by 31 Psychologists

Objective	High school teachers		Psychologists	
	$\overline{X}$	SD	$\overline{X}$	SD
Personal problems	2.40	1.46	4.19	1.74
Scientific knowledge	3.39	2.13	2.35	1.85
Social relationships	3.50	1.71	4.54	1.38
Philosophy of life	3.64	1.80	4.38	1.67
Learning-study	4.10	1.60	3.70	1.59
Family living	4.73	1.49	5.00	1.58
Vocational	6.20	1.25	5.80	1.53

Note. Taken from T. L. Engle, Objectives for subject matter stressed in high school courses in psychology. *American Psychologist*, 1967, **22**, p. 163.

In a very real sense, then, the disagreement between the "personal growth" educators and the disciplinarians may be a split between college-level and precollege educators. Doubtless these differences in priorities reflect adolescent personal-adjustment problems more likely to be a significant part of a high school psychology student's life than that of a college-age psychology student. They also may reflect the more extensive graduate training of college-level educators who have a greater personal and professional investment in the discipline of psychology per se. As previously mentioned, Ross (1972) suggests that psychologists at the college level consistently advocate education based in the facts and findings of their discipline, the communication of scientific knowledge and procedure; most high school teachers simply do not have this fund of information and skills upon which to draw.

For psychologists, psychology is the study of human (and animal) behavior with the ultimate goal of predicting and controlling behavior —control not in a negative sense but in a positive one of promoting human welfare. Among the most stable of psychology's "laws" are those concerning (a) reinforcement: an organism will tend to repeat responses that produce a pleasing state of affairs; (b) frequency: to remember something, repeat it often; (c) novelty: new experiences, if they are not too different from what we are used to, are most positively evaluated (Zajonc, 1970); and (d) "grandmother's law": a high-frequency event may be used as a reinforcer for a low-frequency event (Premack, 1965). Many similar generalizations could be used as illustrations, and many of them could actually be used by the enterprising teacher in enhancing the effectiveness of the teaching process itself. That is, laws of behavior can be applied in the classroom process in teaching psychology and other subjects. Some of these principles are currently being applied to the teaching of psychology, as well as other subjects, in the form of behavior modification (e.g., Sarason, Glaser, & Fargo, 1972), precision teaching (e.g., Johnston & Pennypacker, 1971), contract teaching (e.g., Johnston, 1972; Poppen & Thomson, 1971), and the setting of behavioral objectives (e.g., Mager, 1962).

Let us consider several discipline-based orientations to high school psychology. One is provided in a curriculum guide developed by the Montgomery County (Maryland) Public Schools (1971). Quoting directly from that report:

One may distinguish three basic purposes in statements justifying high school courses in psychology:

1. To aid the student in academic and vocational choice often by textbook coverage of the subject or by familiarization with the enduring ideas and problems of psychology, e.g., through links with literature studies.

2. To teach the student about the investigative approach to behavioral observation, formulation of hypotheses, setting up experimental situations, gathering and analyzing data.

3. To familiarize the student with psychological principles in a human relations or mental health context, e.g., emphasis on peer relations, marriage, parenthood, etc. (p. 1ff.)

McKeachie (1962) offers a second illustration of the discipline-based approach. At the cognitive level, he advocates an attempt to develop curiosity in students regarding the behavior of people, an attempt to develop student curiosity about and appreciation for the use of scientific methodology in the investigation of human behavior, and presentation of the social sciences in a manner that will be both stimulating and appealing to students with the potential to contribute to the social sciences. He avoids suggesting investigation of the "unconscious" behavior of the student or his or her fellow students.

Finally, although claiming a generalist's interest in teaching psychology at precollege levels, Bare (1971) sounded a cautionary note:

No prescription will be offered here and perhaps one should be actively avoided, for society needs both the principles, even if they are difficult to come by, and the solutions, even if they are temporary. One caution may be in order: psychology demands that hypotheses be confirmed, and some of man's most ingenious guesses in science have failed this test and have had to be discarded. (p. 6)

Having professed neutrality, Bare then lists 10 topics that "might have some appeal to the high school student": the split brain, sensory psychophysiology, animal behavior, behavior modification, social learning and imitation, love, Piaget, sleep and dreaming, signal detection, and self-control. Clearly this is still, at heart, a discipline-oriented psychologist speaking.

The advocates say. In support of the discipline-based approach, advocates cite the benefits brought to many areas of practice in real life by application of principles and methods developed in the discipline. Particularly, they point out the usefulness of such applications in teaching. The effectiveness of using the principles of psychology in teaching is supported in innumerable ways. For instance, the value of reinforcement in encouraging children to learn and retain a set of information or procedures has been too frequently documented to require substantiation here. The use of performance contracting, in which the teacher and student specify that work will be required to achieve each of several grades ranging from A to Incomplete or F, has been repeatedly demonstrated to yield better performance in a variety of learning environments than less well-structured, and thereby more ambiguous, environments (e.g., Johnston, 1972). With the use of contract teaching, differences in student interests and motivations can be accommodated without adversely affecting the amount of material learned.

Advocates also argue that there is substantial benefit to a future citizenry informed about the actual nature and methods of psychology and thereby able to apply psychological principles to the solution of individual and societal problems. Not only can these principles be fruitfully applied to problem-solving in such practical fields as teaching, but also, such preparation may make students less gullible to the claims of astrologers, advertisers, and quacks, among others.

Finally, advocates argue that the single most valuable piece of information a student can learn is that behavior is lawful and therefore generally predictable. This is best taught through the discipline-oriented approach.

The critics reply. Mosher and Sprinthall (1970) embarked on their deliberate psychological education at least partly because of student disenchantment with the concepts traditionally presented and discussed in high school psychology courses. Cole (1960) found in a survey that college students typically felt that their high school psychology courses had not prepared them for college study of psychology as well as chemistry or physics courses in high school had prepared them for further study of these fields in college. Klingelhofer (1972, p. 10) decries the "highly verbal, highly conceptual, abstract, and traditional" nature of introductory level psychology as it is typically offered. To the extent it has focused on the discipline, psychology has not, apparently, been very well received by the students.

On a different theme, Combs (1967) states:

> The problem of learning, modern psychologists tell us, always involves two aspects. One is the provision of new information or experience; the other has to do with the individual's personal discovery of the meaning of information FOR HIM. The provision of information

can be controlled by an outsider with or without the cooperation of the learner. It can even be done, when necessary, by mechanical means which do not require a person at all. The discovery of meaning, however, is a quite different matter. This only takes place in people and cannot occur without the involvement of persons in the process. This is the human side of learning. Now, education has done very well with the first of these dimensions. In fact, we are almost exclusively preoccupied with it. Whenever we think about what to do about teaching and learning, we usually conclude that what is needed is more information. So we go on forever adding things; more subjects, . . . more science. This list is practically endless. Yet the dropout with whom we are all concerned is not the product of a system which failed to provide him information. The dropout was told. The trouble is, he never discovered what it all meant. Our failures are almost never failures of information. Rather, they are human problems, breakdowns of personal meaning. (p. 1)

The essence of Combs' final objection is that knowledge without understanding is essentially knowledge without skill. Regardless of the number of facts, without involvement of the individual, all is lost.

A SYNTHESIS

*Our responsibility is less to
assume the role of experts and try
to apply psychology ourselves
than to give it away to the people
who really need it.* —G. A. Miller

Why. By now some moderate discomfort may have been generated by our raising and dismissing issues with a murmured "voila!" and a wave of the pen-filled hand. It must be confessed we have somewhat deliberately engendered and nourished this discomfort. Our efforts have been as deliberate as the oft-quoted statement of Bruner (1960, p. 31): "Any subject can be taught effectively in some intellectually honest form to any child at any stage of development"; and as deliberate as the plea of Combs to involve the person in the process of education.

Support for either of the two preceding approaches all too often seems to come in the form of extreme statements offered with an intensity sometimes appearing to border on religious fervor. Deliberate and extreme statements may win battles, but they lose wars. They give the unthinking "quick and dirty" solutions (that ultimately don't work very well) to the crucial problems of precollege education in psychology that face psychologists, curriculum developers, and teachers alike. It seems reasonable that an appropriate solution is cooperation and compromise—a synthesis of the best of both approaches.

Let us return to a theme developed earlier concerning the goals of precollege instruction in psychology. We asserted that our system of public education is endowed with students of great variety, in terms of both past training and future needs. As one progresses from kindergarten through grade 12, the variety increases. Simultaneously, ongoing social processes increase the diversity of students within each grade. In short, the variety is substantial, and different students have different needs.

The riots (both town and gown) of the middle and late '60s, generated at least partly by the insensitivity of public education to this diversity of students, have given way to a more reflective student body at both the college and precollege levels. "Give it to me now" has yielded to a generation of much more socially conscious and sophisticated students. Indeed, the war issue and the "communication gap" said to exist between the people and their government can be interpreted to have combined to yield a student body more introspective, yet generally more sensitive to fellow human beings. Changing life styles reflected in new sexual mores, new dress habits, and the drug culture and meditative cults as well as evidence of decreasing federal funds for vast social-support projects have added to the changing focus of the current student.

Klingelhofer (1972), as noted previously, has discussed the changing nature of students and the factors responsible for those changes, describing some innovations at the college level brought about at least partly in response to these changes in students. Kulik (1973) notes a marked increase in the number of undergraduate introductory psychology courses that involve students in social service projects off campus. The social service is sometimes provided in the name of relevance, but more basically it is a reflection of why psychology is currently so popular among undergraduates and such a growing discipline at the high school level. Simply put, the "third force" alternative and the return to nature express a student concern for fellow humans and an interest in using psychology to solve some of the perceived ills of society.

Thus, we find a house divided. We find psychology as a discipline offering data and techniques based on the lawfulness of behavior, yet the high-school age students in a position to benefit from these principles are themselves at a point in their own lives when concern for personal adjustment and social adequacy are uppermost. In response to the apparent disparity between the richness of the discipline and the immediacy of student need for assistance in personal adjustment, teachers have traditionally adopted one of the two strategies discussed above in presenting psychology to precollege (especially high school) students. Unlike these two teaching strategies, a synthesis of the best attributes of both techniques is not widely used as a teaching strategy. However, it is not without precedent. Its elements have existed and evolved over many years and represent a compromise in the best sense. The orientation is essentially the study of you and me by me and you with the broad goal of understanding us all a little better.

Theory and technique. The justification for this approach is basically a combination of the theories cited in support of the personal-adjustment and the discipline-based approaches. The recommendation is to take the best from both and apply it to the task at hand. Avila and Purkey (1972) suggest that self-enhancement and reinforcement—the improvement of the self-concept and behavior modification—are closely related and may sometimes even be the same thing. So justification for the present approach resides in the previously discussed rationales; the goal is enhancing both knowledge of the discipline and an understanding of self, and the two are seen as closely related.

In a recent paper, Fox, Girault, Lippitt, and Johnson (1972) developed a concise framework for meaningful social science education. They would involve the social psychologist and the curriculum developer in the creation of a series of projects and concepts of immediate interest and long-range use to the elementary school student. Their argument goes as follows:

> Perhaps most important in our analysis of the learning situation, to which the curriculum must relate, is the issue of relevance to the learner. Understanding and relating to where learners are and how they can become involved is a challenge for socio-psychological analysis. Linking learners to their curriculum environment is a core problem. In working on this challenge we have used the following socio-psychological generalizations . . .
> 1. that to become involved the learner must see connections of the learning task to his own here-and-now life space;
> 2. that much of the support for learning or inhibition of learning comes from the peer group, with its norms, expectations, taboos, and status criteria;
> 3. that confrontation of a concrete problem dilemma is the most involving start-up for most learning sequences;
> 4. that success in learning efforts depends on acquisition of a repertoire of problem-solving tools and skills;
> 5. that "real" learning requires that we focus on the links within the learner between cognitive information, the values and attitudes relevant to that information, and skills of using information, and actualizing the values through plans, commitments, and skilled actions.
>
> This last point emphasizes one type of interdisciplinary integration which we believe is a core aspect of our curriculum and its use by learners. Too often in analysis there is a serious lack of bringing together the analytic or causal process understandings of a problem, the value of policy aspects, and the action implications and action-taking aspects. Diagnosis, evaluation, planning, and action must be part of a meaningful problem-solving or inquiry process. The conceptual tools and methods of social psychology give us a framework for this interdisciplinary integration of the learning task, the content resources of the disciplines, and the psychological world of the learners. (p. 6)

In other words, the student should be directly involved in the learning process both in terms of the starting point of the lesson and its subsequent content. Ultimately, the goal is development of a repertoire of skills and practice in applying the skills to action-oriented situations, thereby increasing the likelihood of transfer to real life.

A different orientation has been adopted by Ross (1972). Aware of the tendency for high school psychology courses to become primarily involved with personal-adjustment problems, Ross designed a course that combines the principles of scientific psychology with student interests. The basic principle underlying the course is that concept formation is facilitated by involving a student with a concept in several different stimulus situations, as advocated by Gagné (1970). The learning-set experiments of Harlow (1949) provide the paradigm. In essence, Ross presents a variety of materials that contain similar underlying psychological concepts and deal with problems directly relevant to student concerns. Through the exposure to numerous such problems students can arrange a large amount of information in terms of the fewer, more generally meaningful, underlying concepts.

The *Instructor's Resource Book,* for the text *Psychology: A Brief Introduction* (Wertheimer, Björkman, Lundberg, & Magnusson, 1971), outlines the goals and objectives of a high school psychology course in terms of applying a few well-chosen principles of the scientific discipline to the development of self-knowledge and competence in dealing with the environment. Specifically, it is stated that

> Introductory courses in psychology have a wide variety of aims. Different teachers, in different settings and with different groups of students, have different objectives. The orientation behind this book is that the purpose of instruction in psychology is to (1) provide the student with basic principles of human behavior and experience, based on empirical facts; (2) show how psychology, as an empirical human science, can be applied in a wide variety of social situations; and (3) provide an objective and differentiated perspective on human beings as individuals and as social creatures.
>
> The key terms in this particular formulation of course objectives are *empirical* and *objective*. Psychology is an empirical science, which implies that it should be presented as a science even in the first introductory course.
>
> Occasionally, inappropriate demands are placed on the field of psychology. By some, psychology is seen as related to the "art of living," involving advice and suggestions on solving personal problems or on sizing up and interacting with one's fellow human beings. ... Much of the material may actually contribute to "self-knowledge." However, self-knowledge does not mean the facile repetition of the latest theories—it means the acquisition of information about principles of human behavior based on scientific methods of observation. (Wertheimer & Holmstrom, 1972, pp. 1-2)

Black/White America (Kasschau, 1974a), a two-week teaching module on race relations, illustrates still another approach faithful to the discipline, yet focusing on a topic of immediate concern to today's student. The philosophy behind the module encourages the teacher to address the "relevant" controversial issues that are of interest to students, but to do so in a manner that protects diversity of opinion, examining evidence and opinions critically rather than using them to support previously held conceptions or to deny alternative views. The teacher is supplied with a variety of concepts and several times as much material as is needed to teach the module's basic lessons in the two weeks for which it is intended. The teaching strategy is that of open investigation:

> *open* in that (1) all topics can be covered, (2) the issue at hand is not resolved, but considered at its present point of development, [and] (3) no approach to investigation is ignored. [It is] *investigative* in that (1) student inquiry is encouraged, (2) a variety of techniques for scrutiny and criticism are developed, and (3) issues are not resolved, but discussed. (p. 2)

The module is interdisciplinary in drawing examples from the provinces of both psychology and sociology. It involves exercises that deal directly with the student milieu, yet it includes suggestions and support materials for the teacher to develop the unit around a variety of themes as determined by local needs and concerns. The *Black/White America* module shares a number of assumptions with the recently initiated APA Human Behavior Curriculum Project:

1. The psychological study of behavior should be the point of departure for the teaching materials.

2. The materials should permit the full consideration of interdisciplinary areas since psychology readily interfaces with sociology (e.g., as in *Black/White America*), biology (e.g., animal behavior), political science (e.g., aggression), and economics (e.g., monetary games) as well as with other fields.

3. Most broadly, the modules should place students in an experiential and conceptual framework that illustrates human interactions and specifically a cause-and-effect analysis of behavior.

The philosophies underlying the projects above (from Lippitt, Fox, & Schaible [1969] to Wertheimer and from Ross to the proposed modules of APA) have within them varied, but consistent, attempts to use the principles of psychology more effectively to communicate the discipline to the student in terms of day-to-day concerns and problems. In a nutshell, the underlying philosophy behind all of them, and the synthesis as advocated here, is that "human behavior can be systematically observed, that it exhibits enough regularity to make possible the derivation of general statements, and that principles of human behavior can be discovered by empirical means that are quite different from mere opinion based on private experience" (Bare, 1973, p. 8). Furthermore, this position maintains that such an approach is likely to be of greatest value to psychology students, at any educational level, for their academic, personal, and social development.

The advocates say. Among the primary virtues of this synthesis is its inherent flexibility. Although the principles of psychology are (relatively) firm and invariant, starting from them in the development of curriculum philosophy, content, and method places little if any restraint on the innovative educator. The assumption is that regardless of the psychological phenomenon discussed, it can ultimately be explained by a variant of the most basic assertion of scientific psychology: behavior is lawful.

There is something in the compromise approach for everyone. This statement of advocacy really has two themes buried within it. First, psychology itself offers principles for how to teach psychology. Second, such an approach can be addressed to a wide variety of topics, whether teacher or student generated.

The critics reply. Critics would point to two major dangers in the attempt to wed cognitive content and skills to the affective aspect of education. First they would claim that there is an inherent incompatibility between the two approaches. The cognitive domain is considered to be public and capable of measurement, whereas:

One's beliefs, attitudes, values, and personality characteristics are more likely to be regarded as private matters—this public-private status of cognitive vs. affective behaviors is deeply rooted in the Judaeo-Christian religion and is a value highly cherished in the democratic traditions of the Western World. (Krathwohl, Bloom, & Masia, 1964, p. 18)

Commenting on this distinction, Sprinthall (1971) notes,

If we can affect people at a value level without reaching them privately then we may have a kind of "sanforized" curriculum that will accomplish the broad objectives of affective/personal education without having the process become personal, emotional or private. (p. 374)

In essence, critics would say that even the best academic content teaching is doomed to remain entirely cognitive, having at best a "coat-tail" effect on the affective domain. The two approaches may be inherently incompatible.

The other danger revolves around the concern of some that society may inappropriately sanction the formulation of a "national curriculum." This was well expressed in a roundtable discussion at a conference on "Social Science in the Schools: A Search for Rationale."

In view of . . . the fact that learning has to be relevant to the student and . . . that learning is something one does, ultimately won't curriculum have to be planned for individual students, or perhaps for individual groups of students? If this is the case, curricular development will have to be done by the schools rather than on a national level. . . .

When you see how excellent materials are used by people who are not prepared to use them, I have the feeling that you have to concentrate on getting people to do something for themselves.

What is needed is to make teachers much more self-educated and self-developing. It is not enough to have good materials and good curricula. (Morrissett & Stevens, 1971, p. 120)

Two issues are raised. The first expresses the fear that national curriculum may be inappropriate because of the individualized nature of learning; this would be a convincing criticism of a single monolithic disciplinarian approach to any sets of facts, psychological or otherwise. The second issue concerns both the nature of curriculum materials and the preparation of teachers to utilize those materials most effectively. It is these topics that form the substance of the next two sections of this document.

Psychology Curriculum Materials

In the decade that generated the Biological Sciences Curriculum Study, the Physical Science Study Committee, Sociological Resources for the Social Studies, and other curriculum projects, psychology failed to follow suit. Before the APA's Human Behavior Curriculum Project was launched, there were within psychology only a few small, locally based curriculum development projects. There were, however, some major national curriculum development projects in other disciplines that incorporated content from psychology. All three approaches discussed in the preceding section are represented in these previously developed materials. In this section we have singled out three sets of psychology curriculum materials for examination, each representing one of the three approaches: personal development, discipline-oriented, and synthesis. The sampling is, of course, meant to be illustrative, not exhaustive. In each case, a description of the curriculum materials and/or teaching process is followed by a brief discussion of the evaluations that have been reported regarding the materials.

PERSONAL DEVELOPMENT

Although still in the formative stages, the curriculum project that has had the greatest impact as a representative of personal development is undoubtedly the "deliberate psychological education" approach of Mosher and Sprinthall (1971). They have developed five separate courses that collectively attempt to focus on personal growth and development in adolescents and young adults. Their goal is "to make personal development the primary, not the secondary, objective of a regular school curriculum" (p. 15). The courses they have developed include (a) a seminar and practicum in peer counseling for high school students; (b) a course in educational psychology that gives high school seniors the opportunity to teach elementary school children under a variety of supervisory situations; (c) a participatory course in improvisational drama, which "affords the individual the opportunity to experience intellectually, physically, and intuitively in order that he explore himself and others in the living, immediate situation" (p. 49); (d) a seminar and practicum in child development, in which students participate in evening seminars tied to daily work in a nursery school; and (e) a course involving the arts and communication.

In order to illustrate what Mosher and Sprinthall have tried to accomplish, let us consider the procedures involved in the peer counseling course. The semester is broken down into three phases of instruction. In the first phase, students are asked to introduce and tell about themselves at length, to relate some recent experiences that have been quite vivid for them, and to prepare some role-play counseling situations sufficiently removed from their own lives to permit independent assessment and criticism of the counseling techniques they are developing. The emphasis here is on carefully supervised practice in role-playing fictional counseling situations.

During the second phase of the course, a noticeable shift in focus begins to occur. According to Mosher and Sprinthall (1971), instead of developing a role-play "character," students begin to present aspects of their own lives in the practice counseling sessions. Each student, during his or her turn as therapist, is soon found to be "counseling" fellow students on the real-life problems of the latter, although the latter is supposed to be role-playing a self-generated "character." During the latter portion of the second phase, Mosher and Sprinthall place increasing emphasis on helping others with less emphasis on self-analysis except as it facilitates development of skill as a counselor.

Mosher and Sprinthall (1971) continue the dual focus of each student both on self and "helping" others as the students enter the third phase of the course. The designers are interested in determining students' ability to translate their understanding of counseling as a form of communication into actual practice. In the final phase, occupying the latter half of the course, the students begin counseling sophomores and juniors who had been identified by the regular high school counselors.

The last phase of the course thus was taken up with continued group supervision of the tapes of actual counseling. The students demonstrated both in the counseling itself and in the discussion of the counseling in the supervision sessions significant ability to listen and respond. (p. 27)

Because the program has developed in the natural school setting, problems of evaluation have been rather complex and hindered by the lack of widely available and established tests to measure "psychological growth" in adolescents. Mosher and Sprinthall had available the class in counseling ($n = 23$) and a regular high school class in psychology ($n = 23$). Students had been randomly assigned to each from the entire group of students signing up for courses in psychology. Both groups were given the Kohlberg Moral Judgment Scale (one half of it on entering the class, the other half on completion) and the Loevinger Sentence Completion Form, a test of ego development. Two other measures were also obtained: (a) unobtrusive and clinical measures, including class attendance and student comments, and (b) for the students in the counseling class, a direct assessment of their counseling skills based on the work of Carkhuff and Berenson (1967). (Despite the use of this latter measure,

Mosher and Sprinthall do note that their primary interest was in personal development of the students in the counseling class rather than the communication of a training method itself.)

The results are consistent in direction, but mixed in significance. Before and after comparisons on the Kohlberg scale yielded a nonsignificant increase in the maturity of judgments for all members of the counseling class. Similar comparisons of data from the Loevinger form indicated a substantial and significant improvement in developmental level. By contrast, the psychology control class yielded no significant improvement or change on the pretest/posttest comparisons of either the Kohlberg scale or the Loevinger form. Regarding counseling skills, results generated from the Carkhuff Counselor Rating Scales, although based on only partial data analysis, indicated significant improvement in overall counselor effectiveness. Finally, and as might be expected, results of interviews with participants yielded very positive statements from students asked to evaluate the counseling course.

In substance, then, although evaluation of the effects of "deliberate psychological education" is difficult, preliminary evidence seems to indicate that the approach does have impact on the students involved in it. A replication effort is underway in the Minneapolis, Minnesota, schools.

PSYCHOLOGY AS A DISCIPLINE

Unlike the courses in "deliberate psychological education," which are aimed at high school seniors, the "Man: A Course of Study" (see Hanley, Whitla, Moo, & Walter, 1970) materials are aimed at the upper elementary (primarily fifth and sixth) grades. The course also has a very different set of goals:

1. To initiate and develop in youngsters a process of question-posing (the inquiry method).
2. To teach a research methodology where children can look for information to answer questions they have raised and use the framework developed in the course . . . and apply it to new areas.
3. To help youngsters develop the ability to use a variety of first-hand sources as evidence from which to develop hypotheses and draw conclusions.
4. To conduct classroom discussion in which youngsters learn to listen to others as well as to express their own views.
5. To legitimize the search; that is to give sanction and support to openended discussions where definitive answers to many questions are not found.
6. To encourage children to reflect on their own experiences.
7. To create a new role for the teacher, in which he becomes a resource rather than an authority. (Hanley et al., 1970, p. 5)

Although the course draws from several disciplines, including psychology, anthropology, and sociology, it serves as a good example of the discipline-centered approach in that it utilizes key concepts from the disciplines as principal organizers.

"Man: A Course of Study" (MACOS) examines several basic questions about the nature of man and the forces that shape humanity: What is human about human beings? How did they get that way? How can they be made more so? The materials begin with studies of the behavior patterns of animals such as salmon, herring gulls, and baboons, and then moves into an extended examination of the life of the Netsilik Eskimos. Emphasized concepts include life cycle, adaptation of organisms, learning, and aggression, with particular attention given to group organization and communication and language. Controversial issues such as reproduction and killing are also considered.

A tremendous variety of materials are provided for student use: films, records, games and simulations, and booklets containing field notes, poems, stories, songs, construction exercises, observation projects, and data in various formats. The variety of materials is intended to foster development of observational and analytical skills. The nine teaching manuals suggest many different strategies and techniques for focusing the materials. Large and small group discussion frequently follows individual research tasks and individual and group projects call upon students to test their generalizations. A training program for teachers, consisting of readings, tapes, and films, has been designed to give teachers a deeper understanding of the teaching approach employed in MACOS.

Just as the course represents a departure from traditional elementary school social studies efforts, the evaluation program developed to test the effectiveness of MACOS is also a departure from tradition. It was felt that the course as a whole "lost an essential quality" when evaluated lesson by lesson. As a result, a series of questions were formulated to address such issues as (a) whether the course helps the students to learn to understand themselves and others in ways they were incapable of prior to the course, (b) whether students are increasingly able to use this new knowledge in and out of the classroom; (c) whether the course is especially effective with particular types of students, and finally, (d) whether teachers' styles of teaching tend to change during the course.

Three basic evaluative techniques were used:

1. The interview method, with semistructured, open-ended, leading questions, was used primarily to assess student opinion of the course. This same procedure turned out to be a valuable means of assessing the effects of the teacher training seminar and the teachers' evaluation of the course.

2. Classroom environment checklists were also developed to get students' responses to the following type of question:

If I had to describe studying the Netsilik Eskimo I would use the words: easy, confusing at times, makes me think, fun, hard, not very important, boring, etc. (Hanley, 1970, p. 21)

3. Tests were used to judge the amount of information absorbed by children, although this particular assessment device was minimized in the evaluation. Written pre- and posttests at the beginning and end of the two sections of MACOS served primarily as measures of group achievement, providing a standard for comparing how children from specific settings and grade levels dealt with the materials.

Some 2,000 students were tested in the formative evaluation of the program. Unfortunately, although the reader is assured that extensive statistical analyses were performed, most of the evaluation results reported in the 1970 publication speak more in terms of the general successes and failures of MACOS than of specific numerical estimates of changes or lack of changes. However, a number of trends do seem well justified by the report.

It seems that the greatest amount of informational learning occurred in the first section of the course, but that progress toward more general goals, such as exchange of views with fellow students and a willingness to explore the total environment, moved at a slower pace, tending to improve as the course continued. The information-test results indicated that in both sections of the course the students made significant gains in learning. Interestingly, testing devices specifically attempting to analyze the effect of the games indicated "that studying past games and planning for future ones improved the learning of most of the kinds of knowledge tested" (Hanley et al., 1970, p. 24).

Comparing the "Man: A Course of Study" classes with similar control classes revealed significant differences in the teaching style employed and the content of the two different classes. The MACOS classes tended to devote more equal amounts of student time to reading texts, watching films, question-and-answer sessions, guided discussion, and writing. By contrast, control groups tended to be much less pupil centered and rely more on the didactic mode of teaching. The evaluators conclude that the evidence supports the claim that "Man: A Course of Study" had succeeded on its own terms.

THE SYNTHESIS

The synthesis offered as a compromise, it will be recalled, aims to enhance both knowledge of the discipline and an understanding of self by presenting psychology in the context of substantive problems that are of vital concern to the precollege student. The American Psychological Association's Human Behavior Curriculum Project (HBCP) has recently initiated development of approximately 30 two-week teaching modules that, in aggregate, might be such a secondary-level course. It is intended that such modules offer high school students an introduction to the study of behavior emphasizing practical examples of psychology in the student's world. As it develops, HBCP has within it sufficient flexibility so that teachers with very different basic training would be able to draw from the project support materials for their particular modes of teaching—both process and content.

Illustrative of these units is the prototypic *Black/White America* module developed by Kasschau (1974a). This module illustrates one method of using the principles of the discipline to facilitate the study of behavior and improve understanding. *Black/White America* is a process-oriented module on majority–minority group relations. It uses a variety of teaching materials and techniques and involves the student in a variety of activities. Specific behavioral objectives are stated at the outset of each lesson and applied in the interest of fostering better relations between the races, based on increased comprehension of social processes.

The teacher who uses the . . . unit will be presented with a table having 10 columns, each with one to eight rows of activities. Each column represents one day, and to teach a two-week unit on minority groups the teachers simply selects one activity from each column, progressing from left to right. This procedure offers 108,864 ways of presenting some very basic points . . . We start with a pre-unit measure of "where the student's at" regarding prejudice and toleration of members of other races. The next couple of days are spent in activities designed to demonstrate to students that they do have prejudices. It includes some activities to sensitize the students to various means by which discrimination is perpetuated.

Still in an information-gathering spirit, the lesson progresses to activities wherein the students are individually gathering information which is collected, analyzed, and discussed in class to reach some additional conclusions. For example, each student might be asked to collect and compare the prices of certain specified food items from stores in ghetto and middle-class neighborhoods. There are also a number of games, classwide experiments, and role-playing situations suggested. The latter stages of the lesson involve group activities oriented toward summarizing the information previously gathered and experienced, analyzing it, understanding it, and thereby understanding what prejudice and discrimination are and how this affects blacks. The final day(s) involve administration of post-unit measures (either then or several weeks later), and also some suggestions are made to the students for ways in which to extend the unit into practice, such as organizing a "People's Fair" for their high school or getting involved as a big brother or a big sister to a ghetto child.

Underlying the development of both units has been the explicit assumption that the principles of the discipline should be related to the everyday world that will be faced by non-collegebound students. (p. 42)

The initial evaluations of the *Black/White America* module were of a formative nature, including only classes that were exposed to the module. Remaining to be analyzed are the more informative comparisons of *Black/White America* classes with comparable control classes. However, with that limitation in mind, the initial formative evaluations, involving over 1,200 students, did reveal some interesting trends and changes in student opinions.

For evaluating the module, three types of tools were developed: First, pre- and postmeasurements were made in 40% of the pilot classes using (a) a modified version of Rotter's Internal/External Control Test (Rotter, 1966), (b) Bogardus' Social Distance Scale, and (c) a simplified method for developing a sociometric analysis of the class. The module would be judged successful if the students tended to become more internally controlled on the Rotter I/E test and less discriminatory in their choices on the Bogardus scale. A similar conclusion would be supported by sociogram data if students showed less consistency in selection of specific class leaders and a lesser tendency to create isolates (i.e., students who are not selected for work projects by any other students). These trends were consistently present in the pilot classes where pre/postmeasures were used. In studying the module, students also tended to show a greater preference for working as part of a small group or with the whole class than was the case in studying other materials. Similarly, the students manifested a slight but significant tendency to prefer to work more without the teacher's help during the study of this unit.

Second, a six-page questionnaire was used to identify those activities in which students felt they learned the most, those that they enjoyed the most, and those on which they worked the hardest. In addition, student perceptions of changes in their own behavior as a result of the module were measured. Student ratings were highest for those activities in which student input played the most significant role in lesson content. There was a positive correlation between the positiveness of student rating of each activity and their rating of the degree of student input to that activity. Conversely, there was a negative correlation between the positiveness of student evaluation of an activity and the degree of teacher input to that activity. Interestingly, listening to others' opinions was also rated as an activity in which students learned most during their study of *Black/White America*. Teachers, generally quite encouraged by the ratings, indicated that they reflected increasing desire for student independence, not negative evaluation of teacher input per se.

Third, a written questionnaire, and in some cases direct telephone interviews, solicited teachers' comments concerning the effects of the unit on their students as well as the ease of teaching the unit. Verbal comments from the teachers were extremely positive in support of the project, its goals, and techniques. As might be suspected because of the pilot nature of the initial development effort, there were occasional negative comments, usually generated from misunderstanding of the purposes of an activity, or philosophical questions about what a specific exercise was intended to convey. Again, overall teacher evaluation of the unit was quite high and very supportive of continued development efforts of a similar nature.

COMMENT

Having presented three illustrative curriculum projects, each intended to demonstrate the application of a particular teaching technique and philosophy in the communication of specific content and/or process knowledge, two comments are in order. First, the current state of evaluation of curriculum development projects is not encouraging. Over and above the inconsistency generated by the widely disparate philosophical launching points for each project, there is widespread lack of regard for establishing appropriate control groups, using previously standardized tests, and consistently reporting the results of these evaluations. The effect of this state of affairs is to lend yet greater value to efforts such as the Social Science Education Consortium's *Data Book* and the periodic special reviews in *Social Education* (both described in Appendix A, pp. 55-57). These efforts represent the only widely circulated, currently available attempts to apply consistent schemes of critical evaluation to a large number of social studies curriculum projects. Their value attests to the need for greater efforts, especially on the part of curriculum developers.

Second, a consistent but questionable feature of various evaluative schemes is the "personal testimony" gathered from participating teachers, which almost always yields a positive evaluation of the project involved. Although it undoubtedly soothes the ego of the curriculum developer, its value to an independent reader is questionable. Moreover, it raises the very real possibility of an interpersonal "Hawthorne" effect, that is, "They're interested in me and my students, so I like what they're doing." If such is the case, the existence of this bias lends yet further support to the need for careful evaluative techniques for precollege psychology.

SOURCES OF INFORMATION REGARDING PSYCHOLOGY-RELATED CURRICULUM MATERIALS

In social and behavioral sciences there is a variety of curriculum materials already in existence. Prior to the recently initiated Human Behavior Curriculum Project, however, there was no national curriculum development project with psychology as its subject matter targeted at secondary school students. As a result, curriculum materials focusing on psychology have been and are scattered far and wide. More often than not, psychology and psychology-related materials are part of curricula focused on other subjects or other disciplines. Psychology is included only as support for the central concerns and techniques of those other disciplines.

Because of the disparate nature and location of psychology-related curriculum materials it was impractical to mount a comprehensive review of those materials in the present document. However, in the last several years a significant number of information sources have evolved that summarize or review curricula or suggest other sources to assist in the teaching of precollege psychology. These survey and critical review sources are listed with annotation in Appendix A of this document.

Teacher Training and Certification

We have reviewed the history and the recent rapid growth of psychology in United States schools. We have examined the two primary philosophical approaches to the process and content of precollege psychology courses, concluding with some suggestions synthesizing the best of each of these into a compromise strategy for teaching psychology. Having developed and documented the value of the synthesis, we have suggested two major areas in which this approach can and should have an impact: the development of curriculum packages to support the teaching of psychology and the training and certification of present and future teachers of psychology. The latter is the subject of this last section of our discussion.

SURVEY RESULTS

A recurrent theme of the literature on teacher preparation for high school psychology instruction is that the typical teacher is inadequately trained in the field. A survey by Engle (1952c) revealed that the average number of semester hours in psychology of high school psychology teachers was 18.5. However, this total included courses in educational psychology and others not directly concentrating upon the subject matter of psychology as such, but required for high school certification in any field. Engle (1955) later warned that unless organized psychology took responsibility for the preparation of adequately trained high school psychology teachers, some other group was likely to do so.

In 1959 Coffield suggested a set of standards for teachers of high school psychology that clearly were far higher than the majority could (or would wish to) meet at the time. In that same year Engle (1960a) surveyed 100 members of the APA Division on the Teaching of Psychology to determine their views on the preparation of teachers for high school psychology. Almost half of them thought psychology should be taught as a science, 29% as a social study, and 23% as either one—a pattern that is in sharp contrast with the preference for a "personal growth" orientation among precollege psychology teachers. Table 2 presents the responses of Engle's sample to a question about which courses should be required and which would be desirable in the preparation of the high school psychology teacher. Once again, the pattern of what at least half of the psychologists considered desirable far exceeded the teachers' actual preparation, a fact which led Engle to question whether many high school teachers of psychology could be induced to secure that amount of training.

TABLE 2 Percentage of Psychologists Recommending Specific Psychology Courses as Minimum and Desirable Preparation for High School Teachers of Psychology

Course	Minimum	Desirable
General introductory	96	97
Experimental	80	89
Tests and measures	68	78
Statistics	63	76
Personal adjustment	58	58
Adolescence	57	67
Social	48	72
Personality	48	70
Child	44	62
Educational	40	54
Learning	39	69
Abnormal	37	53
History of psychology	32	55

Note. Taken from T. L. Engle, Preparation for teaching psychology in high school. *American Psychologist*, 1960a, **15**, p. 354.

Abrams and Stanley (1967) indicated that only about half of the states certified teaching majors in psychology. Fewer than one college in 100 offered a course in methods for teaching psychology, and the opportunities for practice teaching in psychology were meager indeed. They commented that

although only a small minority of the institutions presently offer an undergraduate teaching major in psychology, the large majority of respondents seemed to indicate a willingness to be influenced by [the committee's] findings both by their requests for summaries ... and by their comments that they are especially anxious to see the results. (p. 168)

Basically, the situation of high school psychology is very similar to that of any economically underdeveloped body needing resources to bring about development which can be obtained only after development has begun. A "take-off" is required. (p. 169)

They also wrote:

There is an abundant supply of students who want to be prepared and of institutions that want to prepare them, but this is generally as far as it goes.

There is a long way to go before high-quality high school teachers of psychology will be turned out in large quantities. "Retreading" of already certified teachers during summer sessions may be needed to augment the baccalaureate-level trickle until it becomes more of a torrent. (p. 169)

The findings of Schumacher (1971) in Ohio seem to typify the outcome of more recent surveys. As a follow-up to an earlier study of changes in Ohio high school psychology, between 1966 and 1971 Schumacher surveyed the approximately 300 Ohio high schools listed by the State Department of Education as teaching psychology. Returned were 212 replies. Schumacher comments on the rather poor preparation of high school psychology teachers in Ohio, noting that

> approximately 75% of the teachers currently teaching psychology have had less than 20 semester hours of psychology instruction. When the number of teachers with less than 30 hours of psychology is considered, the figure climbs to approximately 90%. Apparently most high school psychology instructors in Ohio are teaching courses for which they have had minimal direct training. Most psychology teachers are trained in social science. Approximately 80% of all the surveyed teachers had major certification in social science, with other areas (English, physical education and physical science) far behind. (1971, p. 6)

Schumacher also noted that such data further strengthened the conclusion he had drawn from his earlier survey:

> Most teachers of psychology have been trained to teach other content fields and are either asked or volunteer to teach courses in psychology even though they may lack the relevant training. (p. 5)

A bright note was that some 63% of the high schools indicated their willingness to accept student teachers of psychology, making it clear that a critical feature of preservice training for potential high school teachers in Ohio was available at least in terms of written expression of interest. Also encouraging was that over half of the schools reported that their psychology teachers would be interested in attending a summer institute in psychology. Fully 90 of the 212 responding schools indicated that they would presently consider hiring a person to teach psychology "if that person were well trained in the field." Most respondents indicated that the teaching of psychology would only be part time, but over 25 expressed an interest in hiring a full-time psychology instructor.

The present situation is summarized well in two succinct paragraphs by Bare (1973):

> Our limited data (Anderson 1965; Engle 1967; Kremer 1967; McFadden and Pasewark 1970; Parrott and Setz 1970; Schumacher 1971) indicate that the preponderance of high school psychology teachers have come to psychology *de nouveau*, most often with majors and several years' teaching experience in social science/social studies but frequently in other fields entirely. Recent state and regional surveys (Gnagey 1971; Goodale 1970; Hunt, Bodin, Patti and Rookey 1969; McFadden and Pasewark 1970; and Parrott and Setz 1970), though more encouraging than earlier ones, still indicate that the typical high school psychology teacher did not major in psychology as an undergraduate. Of several studies that report on teacher preparation, the highest mean figures are 13.8 undergraduate semester hours, and 19.8 graduate semester hours (Parrott and Setz 1970).
>
> Even such encouraging statistics must be cited with reservation since other studies suggest that hours cited include those areas of psychology required of most teachers for professional education (for example, general psychology, educational psychology, child psychology and adolescent psychology); teacher preparation in experimental psychology appears to be quite limited (cf. Gnagey 1971; Goodale 1970; Kremer 1967). (p. 1)

IMPLICATIONS OF THE THREE TEACHING PHILOSOPHIES FOR TEACHER PREPARATION

Quite aside from the quantity of preservice training in psychology, there is the issue of the focus of that training. Clearly, whether courses in experimental psychology, physiological psychology, statistics and research methodology, sensation and perception, learning, and the like—or in personality, personal development, clinical psychology, mental hygiene, psychopathology—are considered appropriate depends upon the goals chosen by a school for its psychology offerings. If, as appears still to be true in many schools, a primary goal of the high school psychology course is personal growth, self-understanding, emotional openness, and effective interpersonal relations, then, at first sight, courses in the first listed set of areas above might not really be appropriate. Instead, a selection from the second set might be considered desirable, and possibly an exposure to other areas such as sensitivity training, psychiatric social work, and orthopsychiatry (cf. Long, 1971). If, on the other hand, the purpose is to present a balanced view of psychology as an academic discipline, then courses of the kind suggested in the first group above could be considered essential.

The synthesis goal is to present subject matter both in an evidential context and in a manner that demonstrates the personal relevance of the principles to the student's own life. This goal would be more likely to be accomplished by a combination including (a) a firm grounding in the fundamentals of psychology as an empirical behavioral science, that is, in courses of the first kind, preferably with extensive laboratory experiences; (b) some exposure to courses of the second type, as long as there is constant concern for the *evidence* behind each assertion made about "growth," "development," "openness," "mental health," etc.; and (c) exposure to appropriate courses in education (cf. Mosher, 1971) that will help the student teacher relate the principles of general psychology to students' everyday experiences.

Actually, it seems that unless the goal is specified as *only* "personal growth," "mental health," and the like, courses of the second kind above would not really be appropriate at all in the training of teachers of psychology in the schools. Indeed, one can make the case that a firm grounding in the fundamental scientific bases of psychology is essential for any psychology teacher. Preparation only in the "soft" social science or humanistic approach, through some offerings in sensitivity training, mental hygiene, and getting along productively and pleasantly with one's fellow human beings—which runs the risk of having the flavor of absolutism, of religion, of having all the answers—would appear to be a mistake. A teacher who has only this orientation would be doing a disservice to the students since such an approach is a distortion of the field; misrepresents psychology methodologically, epistemologically, and in terms of content; and could even result in psychological distress on the part of some students. It has often been argued that it is unwise for anyone without the requisite training in psychiatry or clinical psychology to engage in the practice of psychiatry or clinical psychology.

At first sight a set of "humanistically" oriented courses might appear appropriate for teachers of courses with the "personal-growth" goal, "solidly scientific" courses for those with the "discipline-oriented" goal, and some of both for those with a combined goal. However, further thought suggests strongly that *all* training for precollege psychology teachers must retain the methodological integrity of psychology as an empirically based discipline, the foundations of which are not personal opinions, subjective feelings, individual experience, or "revealed truth," but rather the dispassionate, objective, measurement-oriented, quantitative approach that also characterizes other scientific disciplines. To be sure, some of the content focus of courses for preparing teachers of psychology and behavioral science in the schools can appropriately be phenomena considered in such areas as motivation, personality, and social psychology, but it is essential that an *evidential* approach be maintained at all times.

This observation would appear to be appropriate whether the training is preservice or inservice. Knowledge of the "hard core" facts, principles, and methods of psychology is, of course, the *sine qua non* of the psychology teacher, otherwise he or she does not have the knowledge that should be imparted to students in a psychology course. Thorough grounding in the subject matter is ideally attained in the preservice years and then maintained during the teacher's career by periodic or continuous inservice updating. Since psychological research is currently making very rapid strides, and since the frontiers of knowledge about basic and applied problems in psychology rapidly are being rolled back, the teacher who desires to remain reasonably up to date must expect to be engaged in constant study of the field. Ideally, time should be provided for enrollment in psychology courses at the university level, or at least for supervised intensive reading in the field, during the teacher's entire career. A less satisfactory alternative would be summer inservice workshops or institutes, at least every five years or so, and preferably every two or three.

IMPLICATIONS FOR TEACHER PREPARATION FROM AVAILABLE CURRICULUM MATERIALS

Many of the newer curriculum materials for teaching psychology in the schools require substantial preservice or inservice teacher preparation; some of them, such as "Man: A Course of Study" (Hanley et al., 1970), demand rather extensive work. Fox, Girault, Lippitt, and Schaible (1967) analyze at some length the problems involved, as seen from the perspective of both curriculum developers and prospective teachers.

A first training step, of course, is to acquaint teachers with what is available—a core purpose of much preservice and inservice training. The ERIC Clearinghouse on Social Studies/Social Science Education, and the Resource and Demonstration Center of the Social Science Education Consortium (SSEC) both serve as depositories for such materials and as disseminators of information about them. Courses on the methodology of teaching psychology can greatly profit from detailed study of the SSEC

(1971) *Data Book* and the APA's (1973) *The Psychology Teacher's Resource Book: First Course*. Any of these alternatives can also be used with profit by the psychology teacher at the middle school and even the elementary school and college levels.

Preservice training can do the job of letting prospective teachers know what is available and how to use it, but inservice training is important for keeping teachers up to date on new materials as they become available. The recent past has seen a major effort to provide better curriculum materials for social science and behavioral science teaching, and there is every indication that this effort is likely to continue, and possibly even intensify, in the near future. The implication is clear: continuing inservice preparation of the psychology teacher is essential, to keep the teacher abreast of new materials in the field, to maintain awareness of new teaching procedures, and to help teachers use the new materials and procedures effectively.

SOME MODEL TRAINING CURRICULA

There are not many programs with a direct, explicit focus on the preservice training of teachers of psychology, but let us glance briefly at a few exemplary models of the kinds of programs that have been proposed or actually implemented, both preservice and inservice, to provide an impression of what is being, or could be, done.

Several years ago, an interdisciplinary group of professors from the College of Education and from various behavioral and social science departments at Illinois State University met frequently to develop a model program for preservice elementary teacher education in social science (Aubertine, 1972). Intended to prepare social science specialists to teach at the fourth to sixth grade level, the program is a fine instance of genuine cooperation among and integration of the efforts of social scientists and educationists. The program consumes most of the four undergraduate years. It is based on a set of assumptions such as the viability of the specialist teacher concept at the upper elementary grades, the desirability of an interdisciplinary thrust, a performance-based structure, individualized instruction, and a community-based orientation. Courses and experience in learning how to teach and in learning appropriate subject matter in the social science disciplines are closely integrated throughout the four years, in three partly overlapping phases. Phase I, "Foundational Experiences," provides background in social science content and methodology, educational philosophy and practice, and child growth and development. Phase II, "Integrating Experiences," concentrates on seminars and applied experiences that broaden perspective over the content of the social sciences and that yield the opportunity for independent study and group projects focusing simultaneously on social science subject matter and how to teach it. Phase III, "Culminating Experiences," requires student teaching, development of a "teaching kit," and seminars on pedagogy, community, and teaching of social science in general.

Long (1972) has developed a very different inservice program intended to introduce elementary teachers to a personal growth curriculum in psychology based on experiential and inductive models of learning. Long tried out the assumptions that unselected sixth-grade teachers could learn, and use comfortably, the methods and materials of her curriculum even if they had not had extensive prior training in psychology. She was interested in determining whether sixth-grade students could learn something about the content and methods of psychology as well as increase their "general psychological comfort," motivation, and performance in the general school curriculum and enhance their self-images. The training program, which involves acquainting the teachers with certain classroom demonstrations and games, helping teachers help students to make relatively dispassionate observations and to draw generalizations from their observations, and observing the teacher at work, apparently resulted in positive gains.

> The carry-over into general teaching method and viewpoint seemed marked and salutary. Doubts that only a psychologist could handle the concepts and materials seemed unsupported. All teachers managed these quite well after varying lengths of time. . . . The teachers in this study repeatedly indicated that their view of their role, of knowledge, and of the children changed remarkably.
>
> Changes in the children's expressed depth of self insight, skills at abstract analysis of behavioral data and view of causality all seem promising and in some cases very significant. (p. 18)

An intensive preservice program for training secondary behavioral science teachers has been instituted at the State University of New York at Plattsburgh (Perkins & Pasti, 1970). The goal of the program is to enhance the effectiveness of the students in the program by making them consumers and disseminators of the information gathered by researchers. The students are intensively involved in research and teaching throughout most of the five-year program. The research training includes behavioral science content and methodology and educational research; the teaching experience includes lecture and laboratory settings in both secondary school and college. Procedures during the training are explicitly intended for subsequent use in the classroom. Summer workshops, an integral part of the program, bring in experienced teachers and provide for interchange of new procedures between these visitors and the students in training. Continuous formative evaluation, including development and use of a structured checklist of skills that characterize the successful secondary behavioral science teacher, is an integral part of the program, which yields a baccalaureate after four years and a master's degree as well as New York state certification after the fifth.

A variant of this thorough five-year approach is to provide an intensive one-year graduate program leading to a master's degree. For students with a substantial background in psychology but no teaching experience, methods of instruction and meeting certification requirements are stressed. For students who are already certified, psychological content is stressed. Such a program has been instituted at New York University by Aileen Schoeppe. Students of both backgrounds take substantial graduate-level work in psychology and share student-teaching experiences. The requirements of mastery include the following courses: educational psychology, survey of developmental psychology, measurement and evaluation, theories of personality, social psychology, experimental psychology, abnormal psychology, and teaching of precollege psychology.

Inservice and continuing education for high school psychology teachers has included (a) brief workshops and symposia held in conjunction with national, state, or regional psychological association meetings; (b) one- or two-day workshops arranged especially for local high school psychology teachers; (c) one-day training sessions conducted by city and county school systems; (d) one- or two-week short courses; and (e) more substantial summer institutes of the kind that the U.S. Office of Education and the National Science Foundation have supported, lasting as long as eight to 10 weeks. The focus of these "retreading" endeavors has been to present some of the latest developments in various research fields, acquaint the participants with new curriculum projects or materials, and/or provide further information on advances in the pedagogical aspects of teaching certain facts, principles, and methods in psychology. Considering the relative isolation of the typical high school psychology teacher, it is to the teacher's advantage to participate in as many workshops and institutes as possible. This provides the opportunity to share experiences and discuss mutual problems with colleagues and to be brought up to date on recent developments in the field, both substantive and pedagogical.

Some viable and promising suggestions have been made for the improvement of both preservice and inservice preparation of psychology teachers in the schools. While a handful of sound teacher preparation programs exist or are in the planning stage, it is still the case that—as Abrams and Stanley (1967) put it—the production of adequately trained psychology teachers for the nation's schools constitutes barely a trickle. This fact was recently reconfirmed by Hunt (1973).

CERTIFICATION OF PSYCHOLOGY TEACHERS

A survey of state departments of education by Johnson (1973b) revealed the following information about certification requirements for high school psychology teachers:

1. Six states and the District of Columbia had no legal provision for teaching psychology. However, one of the states, Tennessee, instituted certification in psychology beginning in Spring 1974.

2. Eight states allowed persons with social studies certification to teach psychology. No further requirements were stated.

3. Six states provided for the teaching of psychology by persons with social studies certification who also had specific preparation in psychology ranging from six semester hours to a major. One additional state, Georgia, had a unique provision for certification in behavioral sciences, granted to persons with specified preparation in psychology, sociology, and anthropology.

4. Twenty-nine states had separate provision for certification in psychology. Requirements ranged from 12 to 34 semester hours, with several states simply specifying a major with no number of hours indicated (Johnson, 1973b).

The specific requirements for each state and the District of Columbia have been assembled in tabular form by Johnson (1973a).

The degree of specificity of the requirements varies enormously from one state to another, and some of the nation's largest states (e.g., New York) do not have specific certification requirements in psychology at all. Perhaps the relative novelty and the rapid growth of psychology in the high schools has contributed to the absence of uniformity in the standards—indeed, to the absence of any standards—in a number of states. Undoubtedly, the establishment of strong yet realistic standards for the certification of high school psychology teachers could do much to help upgrade instruction in our schools. If comparable standards were to prevail in all or most of the states, reciprocity would be a more feasible goal, which in turn could greatly simplify the problems of state certification officials and agencies. Clearly, a national effort to develop guidelines for training and certification is called for. In view of the current concern with accountability, and in view of the empirical orientation of contemporary psychology, it would appear appropriate to suggest that such guidelines be evidentially based. That is, teachers of psychology, and training programs for teachers of psychology, should be evaluated not on the basis solely of the number of semester hours in this course or that, or the philosophical slant of academic experiences, but rather on the basis of demonstrable effectiveness. What can the teacher do? What do the teacher's students actually learn? A competency-based system of teacher training and certification would seem to be particularly appropriate now.

The temptation to list a set of competencies for high school psychology teachers must be resisted here primarily for two reasons. First, as previously noted, the philosophy of psychology that one espouses plays a very direct role in determining the competencies one is likely to deem most appropriate. Therefore, the specification of competencies is a task for which a wide variety of input should be sought and in which premature closure should be avoided.

Second, decisions on training and certification are made primarily at the local and state levels by legislators of varying degrees of knowledge or concern. Thus, although cooperation with national agencies is to be encouraged, the voices of decision should strongly represent local and state constituents who must abide by whatever decision is rendered.

IN SUMMARY

So there you have it—a discipline with a relatively short history which has recently experienced rapid growth at precollege levels. The demand has outstripped our ability to provide fully qualified teachers, but the teachers nonetheless find themselves engaged in fundamental arguments regarding content and technique similar to those that have occupied college-level educators for many years. The main point of the argument is whether personal development or substantive knowledge of psychology as a discipline should be the primary goal. It is suggested here that the argument perhaps should not be resolved in an either–or manner.

While not presuming to resolve the argument, a synthesis has been developed that draws on some of the strengths of the two existing philosophies. We have presented a few samples of curriculum materials currently available and sources of information on other such materials and provided an analysis of teacher training programs (of which there are remarkably few) and current certification requirements.

Appendix A

SOURCES OF INFORMATION REGARDING PSYCHOLOGY-RELATED CURRICULUM MATERIALS

The following sources, with some overlap, contain information about currently available curriculum materials for teaching psychology to secondary school students. The annotations accompanying each source indicate whether that source includes critical reviews or focuses on how-to-do-it information.

American Psychological Association. *The psychology teacher's resource book: First course* (2nd ed.). Washington, D.C.: Author, 1973.

Oriented specifically to the high school teacher of psychology and behavioral science, this book is the single most comprehensive available source of helpful hints, book reviews, lists of equipment and other teaching resources, and lists of publishing and manufacturing organizations. Yielding to very few biases, the information included is so comprehensive as to allow the philosophical and teaching preferences of the individual teacher and/or school district to be more than adequately reflected. The comprehensiveness of this source is well documented simply by annotating its table of contents:

"Reviews of Introductory Textbooks": The reviews cover about 50 currently available textbooks reflecting a wide range of emphases, content, and reading levels. The single major problem with this section is that each review is the product of only one reviewer and as such may reflect some biases.

"Reviews of Books of Readings": Included here is a lengthy list of readings books that might supplement primary teaching texts. Reviewers were asked to address their comments generally to the number of selections, reading level, level of sophistication required of the (high school) student, interest value to such students, and unusual features.

"Reviews of Laboratory Manuals": This section includes a topical listing of about 20 manuals. For example, a group of manuals emphasizing operant conditioning is listed; another list indicates those that demand extensive statistics for successful use, and so on.

"Psychological Periodicals for the High School": Provided here is a relatively complete list of periodicals with psychological content that might be appropriate for the precollege level—those published by the American Psychological Association and also those published by other associations and firms. Marked for specific attention are 13 periodicals judged most suitable for the high school audience. Subscription costs and a general categorization of the journals and their content are offered.

"Novels, Case Studies, Biographies, and Other Popular Books": This section is an annotated bibliography of nontechnical, paperback books broadly related to psychology. The books are arranged in topical categories.

"Audiovisual Materials": Included in this section is a broad-ranging list of selected films as well as videotape, slide, and audiotape series. The list is partially annotated and followed by the addresses of sources and distributors.

"Reference Materials": This section suggests currently available books and articles that a high school instructor might use to supplement the usual sources of information. The books are organized according to their emphases on topics such as "language" and "drugs and behavior."

"Equipment, Animals, and Supplies": Included here is a substantial list of manufacturers of psychological equipment as well as the types of equipment they produce. Also included are lists of dealers in animals and animal supplies as well as a suggested list of books and pamphlets concerning equipment, animals, and animal care.

"Addresses of National Organizations": Detailed here is a wide range of national organizations that will supply information on various subjects of interest to high school psychology students. Such information ranges from sources of consultation on personal problems to sources of formal training opportunities and the availability of funds for teachers.

"Some Ways of Increasing Student Involvement": This section provides teaching hints, including a number of alternative or supplementary suggestions for modification of standard lectures. It also discusses problems of evaluation and measurement and describes a few classroom demonstrations and activities.

"Some Ways of Organizing Instruction": The last section presents three more extensive examples of the manner in which a psychology course could be organized. The emphasis is on "relevance" and on encouraging teachers to organize instruction at the course, rather than topic, level.

"Appendix": Addresses are given for all publishers whose books are cited in the main body of the Resource Book.

Social Science Education Consortium. *Social studies curriculum materials: Data book.* Boulder, Colo.: Author, 1971.

The *Data Book* is a useful innovation in curriculum analysis and evaluation. The materials described in the *Data Book* are of four types: project materials, textbooks, games and simulations, and supplementary materials. (Soon to be added is a section on teacher resource materials.) The *Data Book* was first published in 1971. Two supplements per year keep it up to date by modifying descriptions of materials already included and describing new materials as they are developed. The philosophy behind the book is clearly expressed in the Introduction:

Our objective is to provide analyses of curriculum materials which will allow administrators, curriculum coordinators, college methods teachers, and elementary and secondary school teachers to select materials which are appropriate to their students, school and community on the basis of grade level, discipline, underlying philosophy, goals, strategies, structures, content innovativeness, and merit.

Included in the review of each set of materials is an overview of its significant features, a description of the format, information regarding required teaching time, a description of the student and teacher characteristics necessary for successful use, an explanation of the rationale and general objectives, a description of content, an explanation of the primary teaching procedures, and evaluative data, comments and suggestions for use.

Social Science Education Consortium and National Council for the Social Studies. Evaluation of curriculum projects, programs and materials. *Social Education*, 1972, 36, 712–793.

This special issue of *Social Education* updates an earlier materials review effort by Sanders and Tanck, in 1970. The issue opens with a description of a systematic process for selecting curriculum materials for use in specific school situations. This is followed by an introduction to and overview of the curriculum materials analyzed in the issue. The bulk of the report consists of reviews of 26 social studies curriculum project materials, ranging from psychology to economics to American history. Each review is cast in the same format, covering (in order) product characteristics, rationale and objectives, content, methodology, conditions for implementation, and evaluation. Next is a general article on the selection and evaluation of new social studies materials; of particular value in this article are three forms for teacher evaluation of new materials before and after classroom tryout and a student questionnaire for evaluation of materials. The last article of the series contains a very extensive and briefly annotated list of available supplementary teaching materials ranging from three-dimensional objects, print packages, slides, and sound materials to combined sound-and-sight materials, books, and games and simulations. Although there is no guarantee that *Social Education* will continue to update this valuable series, it is worth keeping an eye on the journal as a source of current information.

Woods, P. J. (Ed.) *Source book on the teaching of psychology.* Roanoke, Va.: Scholars' Press, 1973.

This extensive publication developed from the Course Outlines Project of the American Psychological Association's Division on the Teaching of Psychology, a project that spanned more than 10 years. Published in looseleaf form like the Social Science Education Consortium's *Data Book*, the *Source Book* is intended for the teacher of undergraduate and/or high school psychology. It includes approximately 40 course outlines and bibliographies for teaching in 14 of the traditional areas of psychology and some topical areas of current interest including behavior modification, community mental health, professional problems, psychology and politics, and womankind. Also like the *Data Book*, the *Source Book* will be updated with annual supplements.

Appendix B

BIBLIOGRAPHY OF BIBLIOGRAPHIES

Of the following bibliographies, some were one-time-only efforts, but others, as noted, are periodically revised and updated. There is substantial overlap in the bibliographies, but most have some unique references to offer.

APA Clearinghouse on Precollege Psychology and Behavioral Science. Inventory [of Clearinghouse holdings of the literature on high school psychology]. Unpublished bibliography, 1973. The inventory lists approximately 200 articles and publications that are on deposit in the APA Clearinghouse. Many items that appear on the inventory also appear in three separate bibliographies available from the Clearinghouse. All three carry the main title "Teaching of Psychology in the Secondary School" and are subtitled, respectively, "Studies and Surveys: 1964-1973" (currently 31 references), "Teacher Preparation and Certification" (currently 12 references), and "Course Descriptions, Curriculum Guides, and Instructional Units" (currently 47 references). Whereas the inventory does not indicate where fugitive items may be obtained, the three separate bibliographies do. Both the inventory and the three bibliographies are periodically updated.

Noland, R., & Bardon, J. I. Supplementary bibliography on teaching psychology and the behavioral sciences in the schools. *Journal of School Psychology*, 1967, **5**, 257–260. Noland and Bardon's is a rather comprehensive bibliography that includes a number of the historical papers preceding the special 1967 issue of the *Journal of School Psychology*, of which it is a part. The word "supplementary" in the title means that the bibliography does not duplicate any of the references already cited by authors of articles in the special issue. Both this item and the Schoeppe bibliography encompass elementary school behavioral science as well as high school psychology.

Partin, R. L. Teaching high school psychology: A bibliography. Unpublished bibliography, 1973. (Available on request from the author, Ottawa Hills High School, 2532 Evergreen Road, Toledo, Ohio 43615.) This bibliography contains 107 references concerning all aspects of high school psychology ranging from teacher training to science fair projects.

Schoeppe, A. Teaching psychology and the behavioral sciences in the schools: 1966-1970. *Journal of School Psychology*, 1971, **9**, 303–309. This bibliography supplements the Noland and Bardon one, covering the 1966-1970 period. It also notes some pre-1966 articles not covered by Noland and Bardon.

References

Abrams, A. M., & Stanley, J. C. Preparation of high school psychology teachers by colleges. *American Psychologist,* 1967, **22**, 166–169.
American Psychological Association. *The psychology teacher's resource book: First course.* Washington, D.C.: Author, 1973.
Anderson, R. L. Psychology in Michigan's high schools. *American Psychologist,* 1965, **20**, 169.
Aubertine, H. E. *A model elementary teacher education program for social science majors: An interdisciplinary approach.* Bloomington, Ill.: Illinois State University, October 1972. (Mimeo)
Avila, D., & Purkey, W. Self-theory and behaviorism: A rapproachement. *Psychology in the Schools,* 1972, **9**, 124–126. (ERIC Document Reproduction Service No. EJ 058 205)
Bare, J. K. *Psychology: Where to begin.* Washington, D.C.: American Psychological Association; and Boulder, Colo.: ERIC Clearinghouse for Social Studies/Social Science Education, 1971. (ERIC Document Reproduction Service No. ED 055 938)
Bare, J. K. Secondary school curriculum project on human behavior: A proposal to the National Science Foundation. Washington, D.C.: American Psychological Association, February 20, 1973. (Mimeo)
Bare, J. K., et al. *Program on the teaching of psychology in the secondary school: Final report.* Washington, D.C.: American Psychological Association, 1970.
Belenky, R. Guidance and the teaching of high school psychology. *Community Mental Health Journal,* 1966, **2**, 41–46.
Branca, A. A. *Psychology: The science of behavior* (2nd ed.). Boston: Allyn & Bacon, 1968.
Bronson, J. A. The determination of a course in psychology for the high schools. Unpublished doctoral dissertation, University of Cincinnati, 1932.
Bruner, J. S. *The process of education.* Cambridge, Mass.: Harvard University Press, 1960.
Bryant, P. E., & Trabasso, T. Transitive inferences and memory in young children. *Nature,* 1971, **232**, 456–458.
Bunch, M. Committee on the teaching of psychology in high schools. Report to Education and Training Board, American Psychological Association, May 7, 1954. (Mimeo)
Bunch, M. Committee on the teaching of psychology in high schools. Report to Education and Training Board, American Psychological Association, April 23, 1955. (Mimeo)
Burnes, A. J. Laboratory instruction in the behavioral sciences in the grammar school. In B. Gertz (Ed.), *Behavioral sciences in the elementary grades.* Cambridge, Mass.: Lesley College, Second Annual Graduate Symposium, 1966.
Burnett, C. W. Students' reactions to general psychology course. *California Journal of Educational Research,* 1952, **3**, 25–30.
Carkhuff, R. R., & Berenson, B. G. *Beyond counseling and therapy.* New York: Holt, Rinehart & Winston, 1967.
Coffield, K. E. Suggested standards for teachers of high school psychology. *Bulletin of the National Association of Secondary School Principals,* 1959, **43**, 200–203.
Coffield, K. E., & Engle, T. L. High school psychology: A history and some observations. *American Psychologist,* 1960, **15**, 350–352.
Coffield, K. E., Engle, T. L., McNeely, P., & Milton, O. High school psychology and science fairs. *American Psychologist,* 1960, **15**, 318.
Cole, D. L. A survey of student reaction to high school "psychology." *California Journal of Educational Research,* 1960, **11**, 130–133.

REFERENCES

Combs, A. W. Humanizing education: The person in the process. Paper presented at the 22nd Annual ASCD Conference, Dallas, March 1967.
Crouter, F. Biological prerequisites for teaching introductory psychology. *School Science and Mathematics*, 1956, **56**, 559; 563.
Elliott, L. H. Teaching for life adjustment. *Elementary School Journal*, 1950–51, **51**, 152–156.
Engle, T. L. Psychology—for Michigan City seniors. *Clearing House*, 1939, **14**, 49–51.
Engle, T. L. *Psychology: Its principles and applications*. New York: Harcourt, Brace, 1945.
Engle, T. L. An analysis of high school textbooks of psychology. *School Review*, 1950, **58**, 343–347.
Engle, T. L. A national survey of the teaching of psychology in high school. *School Review*, 1951, **59**, 467–471.
Engle, T. L. Attitudes of teachers and pupils toward a high school course in psychology. *Bulletin of the National Association of Secondary School Principals*, 1952, **36**, 145–151. (a)
Engle, T. L. Teaching of psychology in high schools. *American Psychologist*. 1952, **7**, 31–35. (b)
Engle, T. L. The training and experience of high school teachers of psychology. *Educational Administration and Supervision*, 1952, **38**, 91–96. (c)
Engle, T. L. Some trends in and problems presented by the teaching of psychology in high schools. *Psychological Reports*, 1955, **1**, 303–306.
Engle, T. L. Preparation for teaching psychology in high school. *American Psychologist*, 1960, **15**, 353–355. (a)
Engle, T. L. Preparation for teaching psychology in high school. *Bulletin of the National Association of Secondary School Principals*, 1960, **44**, 171–174. (b)
Engle, T. L. Objectives for and subject matter stressed in high school courses in psychology. *American Psychologist*, 1967, **22**, 162–166. (a)
Engle, T. L. Teaching psychology at the secondary level: Past, present, and possible future. *Journal of School Psychology*, 1967, **5**, 168–176. (b)
Engle, T. L., & Snellgrove, L. *Psychology: Its principles and applications* (5th ed.). New York: Harcourt, Brace & World, 1969.
Engle, T. L., & Snellgrove, L. *Psychology: Its principles and applications* (6th ed.). New York: Harcourt Brace Jovanovich, 1974.
Erikson, E. H. *Childhood and society*. New York: Norton, 1950.
Fox, R., Girault, E., Lippitt, R., & Johnson, P. *A framework for social science education*. Boulder, Colo.: Social Science Education Consortium, 1972.
Fox, R., Girault, E., Lippitt, R., & Schaible, L. *Inservice teacher education to support utilization of new social science curricula*. Boulder, Colo.: Social Science Education Consortium, 1967.
Gagne, R. M. *The conditions of learning* (2nd ed.). New York: Holt, Rinehart & Winston, 1970.
Geisel, J. B. Mental hygiene in the high school. *Phi Delta Kappan*, 1938, **20**, 186–187.
Geisel, J. B. Alumni opinions concerning a high school course in mental hygiene. *Mental Hygiene, New York*, 1940, **24**, 419–433.
Geisel, J. B. Mental hygiene in the high school curriculum. *Bulletin of the National Association of Secondary School Principals*, 1943, **27**, 82–98. (a)
Geisel, J. B. *Personal problems and morale*. Boston: Houghton Mifflin, 1943. (b)
Gertz, B. (Ed.) *Behavioral science in the elementary grades*. Cambridge, Mass.: Lesley College, Second Annual Graduate Symposium, 1966.
Gertler, D. B., & Barker, L. A. *Patterns of course offerings and enrollments in public secondary schools. 1970–71*. Washington, D.C.: U.S. Government Printing Office, 1972.
Gordon, S. *Psychology for you*. New York: Oxford Book Co., 1972.
Hampton, J. D. High school psychology in Oklahoma. *Psychology in Oklahoma*, 1973, **15**, p. 5.

Hanley, J. P., Whitla, D. K., Moo, E. W., & Walter, A. S. *Curiosity, competence, community.* Cambridge, Mass.: Education Development Center, 1970. (ERIC Document Reproduction Service No. ED 045 461)

Harlow, H. F. The formation of learning sets. *Psychological Review*, 1949, **56**, 51–65.

Harris, R. S. Psychology in the high school. *School and Community*, 1939, **25**, 62–63.

Hertzman, J. Developing a mental-hygiene curriculum in a public school system. *Mental Hygiene*, 1952, **36**, 569–588.

Hollister, W. G. An overview of school mental health activities. *Journal of School Health*, 1966, **36**, 114–117.

Hunt, R. G. Programs for training high school teachers of psychology. Paper presented at the Annual Meeting of the American Psychological Association, Montreal, August 1973.

Hunt, R. G., Davol, S. H., & Schoeppe, A. A proposal for precollege psychology and behavioral science. *JSAS Catalog of Selected Documents in Psychology*, 1972, **2**, 49. (Ms. No. 124)

Inhelder, B., & Piaget, J. *The growth of logical thinking from childhood through adolescence.* New York: Basic Books, 1958.

Ivey, A. E., & Alschuler, A. S. (Eds.) Psychological education: A prime function of the counselor. *Personnel and Guidance Journal*, 1973, **51**, 586–691.

Jersild, A. T., & Helfant, K. *Education for self-understanding: The role of psychology in the high school program.* New York: Bureau of Publications, Teachers College, Columbia University, 1953.

Johnson, M. Certification requirements for teaching psychology in United States secondary schools, Spring 1973. *Periodically*, October 1973, pp. 3–4. (a)

Johnson, M. Certification requirements for teaching the behavioral sciences in the secondary schools and their implications for training. Paper presented at the Annual Meeting of the American Psychological Association, Montreal, August 1973. (b)

Johnston, J. M. Performance criteria and college student academic performance. Teaching/Learning Seminar address at the University of South Carolina, Fall 1972.

Johnston, J. M., & Pennypacker, H. S. A behavioral approach to college teaching. *American Psychologist*, 1971, **26**, 219–244. (ERIC Document Reproduction Service No. EJ 045 060)

Kasschau, R. A. *Black/White America: A two-week unit on race relations.* Columbia: University of South Carolina, 1974. (Mimeo) (a)

Kasschau, R. A. Teaching psychology before college: Why, when, and how. *New York University Education Quarterly*, 1974, **5**, in press. (b)

Kasschau, R. A., & Michael, T. D. Psychology in South Carolina high schools in 1973: A survey of teachers. Columbia, S.C.: University of South Carolina, 1973. (Mimeo)

Klingelhofer, E. L. Psychology and the new student. *Teaching of Psychology Newsletter*, March 1972, pp. 8–10.

Klugh, H. E., Deterline, W. A., & Henderson, D. C. A note on the teaching of Skinner's descriptive behaviorism in the fifth grade. *Journal of Educational Psychology*, 1960, **51**, 74–75.

Kohlberg, L. Stage and sequence: The cognitive-development approach to socialization. In D. A. Goslin (Ed.), *Handbook of socialization theory and research.* Chicago: Rand McNally, 1969.

Krathwohl, C., Bloom, B., & Masia, B. *Taxonomy of educational objectives: Handbook II, affective domain.* New York: David McKay, 1964.

Kuhn, T. S. *The structure of scientific revolutions.* International Encyclopedia of Unified Science, 1970, **2**, 1–210.

Kulik, J. A. *Undergraduate education in psychology.* Washington, D.C.: American Psychological Association, 1973.

Lippitt, R., Fox, R., & Schaible, L. *Social science laboratory units.* Chicago: Science Research Associates, 1969.

REFERENCES

Long, B. E. Human relations: Helping your students develop greater self-knowledge and human awareness. *Grade Teacher*, 1971-1972, **89**, September–May.

Long, B. E. Implications of a teacher training program developed for a curriculum in psychology: Elementary school level. *JSAS Catalog of Selected Documents in Psychology*, 1972, **2**, 80. (Ms. No. 177)

Louttit, C. M. Psychology in nineteenth century high schools. *American Psychologist*, 1956, **11**, 717.

Mager, R. F. *Preparing instructional objectives*. Belmont, Calif.: Fearon Publishers, 1962.

Markman, B. S. *High school psychology unit on reinforcement*. Detroit: Wayne State University, 1973. (Mimeo)

McCall, A. B. Psychology, schools and you. *Woman's Home Companion*, 1936, **63**, 30; 38.

McCall, A. B. *Psychology in our schools*. New York: Crowell, 1937.

McKeachie, W. J. Psychology. In American Council of Learned Societies and National Council for Social Studies, *The social studies and the social sciences*. New York: Harcourt, Brace & World, 1962.

McNeely, P. R. Psychology at the secondary school level in Pennsylvania. *The Pennsylvania Psychologist*, July, 1967, p. 5.

McNiel, B. Development at the youth level of a conception of causes and behavior and the effectiveness of a learning program in this area. *Journal of Experimental Education*, 1944, **13**, 81; 85.

Merrifield, P. R., & Schoeppe, A. Report of the Psychology for Youth Conference for High School Teachers of Psychology. New York: New York University, 1969. (Mimeo)

Miller, G. A. Psychology as a means of promoting human welfare. *American Psychologist*, 1969, **24**, 1063–1075.

Montgomery County Public Schools. *Course of study for the high school psychology elective: Working copy*. Rockville, Md.: Author, 1971.

Moore, H. K. Advent of psychology as a unit in junior high school science. *Science Education*, 1932, **16**, 199–200.

Morgan, M. I., & Ojemann, R. H. The effect of a learning program designed to assist youth in an understanding of behavior and its development. *Child Development*, 1942, **13**, 181–194.

Morrissett, I. (Ed.) *Concepts and structure in the new social science curricula*. New York: Holt, Rinehart & Winston, 1967.

Morrissett, I., & Stevens, W. W., Jr. (Eds.) *Social science in the schools: A search for rationale*. New York: Holt, Rinehart & Winston, 1971. (ERIC Document Reproduction Service No. ED 046 847)

Mosher, R. L. Objectives of training programs for secondary school teachers of psychology. Paper presented at the Annual Meeting of the American Psychological Association, Washington, D.C., September 1971. (ERIC Document Reproduction Service No. ED 070 682)

Mosher, R. L., & Sprinthall, N. A. Psychological education in secondary schools: A program to promote individual and human development. *American Psychologist*, 1970, **25**, 911–924. (ERIC Document Reproduction Service No. EJ 042 111)

Mosher, R. L., & Sprinthall, N. A. Deliberate psychological education. *Counseling Psychologist*, 1971, **2**, 3–82.

Noland, R. L. A century of psychology in American secondary schools. *Journal of Secondary Education*, 1966, **41**, 247–254. (a)

Noland, R. L. Shall we teach psychology in the secondary school? *Catholic School Journal*, 1966, **66**, 53–56. (b)

Noland, R. L. School psychologists and counselors view the role of the high school psychology course. *Journal of School Psychology*, 1967, **5**, 177–184.

Noland, R. L., & Bardon, J. I. Supplementary bibliography on teaching psychology and the behavioral sciences in the schools. *Journal of School Psychology*, 1967, **5**, 257–260.

REFERENCES

Ojemann, R. H. Research in planned learning programs and the science of behavior. *Journal of Educational Research*, 1948, **42**, 96–104.

Ojemann, R. H. The effect of an integrated plan for teaching human behavior in schools. *American Psychologist*, 1949, **4**, 217.

Ojemann, R. H. An integrated plan for education in human relations and mental health. *Journal of the National Association of Deans of Women*, 1953, **16**, 101–108.

Ojemann, R. H. *Developing a program for education in human behavior*. Iowa City, Iowa: State University of Iowa, 1959.

Ojemann, R. H., Nugent, A., & Corry, M. Study of human behavior in the social science program. *Social Education*, 1947, **11**, 25–28.

Patti, J. B. Elementary psychology for eighth graders? *American Psychologist*, 1956, **11**, 194–196.

Pechstein, L. A., & Bronson, J. A. The determination of a course in psychology for the high school. *School Review*, 1933, **41**, 356–361.

Perkins, H. J., & Pasti, G. Experimental 5-year program in the preparation of secondary teachers in the behavioral sciences (Proposal submitted to the National Science Foundation). Plattsburgh, N.Y.: State University of New York, 1970. (Mimeo)

Piaget, J. *The origins of intelligence in children*. New York: International Universities Press, 1952.

Pietrofesa, J. J. A course in personal adjustment. *Catholic School Journal*, 1968, **68**, 66–67.

Poppen, W. G., & Thomson, C. L. Effect of grade contracts on student performance. *Journal of Education Research*, 1971, **64**, 420–424. (ERIC Document Reproduction Service No. EJ 040 114)

Premack, D. Reinforcement theory. In D. Levine (Ed.), *Nebraska Symposium on Motivation* (Vol. XIII). Lincoln: University of Nebraska Press, 1965.

Rappaport, J., & Sorensen, J. Teaching psychology to disadvantaged youth: Enhancing the relevance of psychology through public education. *Journal of School Psychology*, 1971, **9**, 120–126. (ERIC Document Reproduction Service No. EJ 045 031)

Ratner, S. C. The role of psychology in the traveling science teacher program for high schools. *American Psychologist*, 1961, **16**, 702–704.

Riddle, E. M. Psychology by request. *High School Journal*, 1939, **22**, 275–277.

Roback, A. A. Psychology in American secondary schools in the 90's. *American Psychologist*, 1952, **7**, 44–45.

Roen, S. R. The behavioral sciences in the primary grades. *American Psychologist*, 1965, **20**, 430–432.

Roen, S. R. The study of behavior by children. In B. Gertz (Ed.), *Behavioral sciences in the elementary grades*. Cambridge, Mass.: Lesley College, Second Annual Graduate Symposium, 1966.

Roen, S. R. Teaching the behavioral sciences in elementary grades. *Journal of School Psychology*, 1967, **5**, 205–216.

Rosenthal, S. A fifth grade classroom experiment in fostering mental health. *Journal of Child Psychiatry*, 1953, **2**, 302–309.

Ross, R. J. A conceptual program for high school psychology. *Psychology in the Schools*, 1972, **9**, 418–422.

Rotter, J. B. Generalized expectancies for internal versus external control of reinforcement. *Psychological Monographs: General and Applied*, 1966, 80(1), 1–28.

Salisbury, W. S. Vitalizing the social studies in the high school. *Education*, 1936, **56**, 618–621.

Sandberg, J. H. *Introduction to the behavioral sciences: An inquiry approach*. New York: Holt, Rinehart & Winston, 1969.

Sanders, N. M., & Tanck, M. L. A critical appraisal of twenty-six national social studies projects. *Social Education*, 1970, **34**, 381–449. (ERIC Document Reproduction Service No. EJ 018 397)

Sarason, I. G., Glaser, E. M., & Fargo, G. A. *Reinforcing productive classroom behavior: A teacher's guide to behavior modification.* New York: Behavioral Publications, 1972. (ERIC Document Reproduction Service No. ED 042 061)

Schumacher, G. M. High school psychology in Ohio, 1966-1971. *Ohio Psychologist*, **18**, 1971, pp. 5–6.

Senesh, L. 1973: A challenge to social science education. Paper presented at meeting of the California Council for the Social Studies in San Francisco, November 1973.

Sigel, I., & Water, E. Child development and social science education, Part III. *Abstracts of relevant literature.* Detroit: Palmer Institute, 1966.

Skaggs, E. B. Psychological studies in the grades and high school. *School and Society*, 1937, **46**, 598–599.

Snellgrove, L. Construction and use of inexpensive psychological apparatus. Jackson, Tenn.: Union University, 1962. (Mimeo)

Social Science Education Consortium. *Social studies curriculum materials: Data book.* Boulder, Colo.: Author, 1971.

Social Science Education Consortium and National Council for the Social Studies. Evaluation of curricular projects, programs, and materials. *Social Education*, 1972, **36**, 712–793.

Solvertz, F., & Lund, A. Some effects of a personal development program at the fifth grade level. *Journal of Educational Research*, 1956, **49**, 373–378.

Sorensen, H., Malm, M., & Forehand, G. A. *Psychology for living* (3rd ed.). New York: McGraw-Hill, 1971.

Sprinthall, N. A. A program for psychological education: Some preliminary issues. *Journal of School Psychology*, 1971, **9**, 373–381.

Stahl, R. J., & Casteel, J. D. *The status of precollege psychology in the state of Florida during 1970-71 and 1972-73: A comparative report.* (Research Monograph No. 8) Gainesville, Fla.: University of Florida, P. K. Yonge Laboratory School, 1973.

Stanley, J. C., & Abrams, A. M. Certification of psychology majors for the public schools. *Psi Chi Newsletter*, Spring 1965, pp. 11–12.

Stone, C. P., & Watson, G. Report of the committee to study problems connected with the teaching of psychology in high schools and junior colleges. *Psychological Bulletin*, 1936, **33**, 709–714.

Stone, C. P., & Watson, G. Survey on teaching psychology in secondary schools. *Psychological Bulletin*, 1937, **34**, 660–674.

Thornton, B. M., & Colver, R. M. The psychology course in secondary schools. *Journal of School Psychology*, 1967, **5**, 185–190.

Thornton, B. M., & Williams, B. J. High school psychology courses in Florida. *American Psychologist*, 1971, **26**, 1040.

Turney, A. H., & Collins, F. I. An experiment in improving the personality of high-school seniors. *Journal of Educational Psychology*, 1940, **31**, 550–553.

Walker, E. I., & McKeachie, W. J. *Some thoughts about teaching the beginning course in psychology.* Belmont, Calif.: Brooks/Cole, 1967.

Wertheimer, M., Björkman, M., Lundberg, I., & Magnusson, D. *Psychology: A brief introduction.* Glenview, Ill.: Scott, Foresman, 1971.

Wertheimer, M., & Holmstrom, M. *Instructor's resource book for Psychology: A brief introduction.* Glenview, Ill.: Scott, Foresman, 1972.

Williams, D. L. Consultation: A broad, flexible role for school psychologists. *Psychology in the Schools*, 1972, **9**, 16–21. (ERIC Document Reproduction Service No. EJ 053 563)

Wright, G. S. *Subject offerings and enrollments in public secondary schools.* Washington, D.C.: U.S. Government Printing Office, 1965.

Zajonc, R. Brainwash: Familiarity breeds comfort. *Psychology Today*, February 1970, pp. 32–35; 60–64.